NEW ENLARGED 1977 EDITION

THE 'OFFICIAL'

CB

SLANGUAGE
LANGUAGE
DICTIONARY

INCLUDING CROSS-REFERENCE

BY

LANIE DILLS

EDITED BY DOT GILBERTSON
AND
JOAN WHEELER

LANIE DILLS • NASHVILLE, TENNESSEE
PUBLISHER

DEDICATION

To: Tim
Cita
Real Friends
Close Family

1977 Edition
© Lanie Dills, 1976

First Edition
© Lanie Dills, 1975
First printing—December 1975
Second printing—January 1976

1976 Edition
© Lanie Dills, 1976
First printing—March 1976
Second printing—March 1976
Third printing—April 1976
Fourth printing—June 1976

Library of Congress Catalog Card Number: LC 76-43636
ISBN 0-916744-01-9
Printed in the United States of America

TABLE OF CONTENTS

INTRODUCTION

Recognizing that CB jargon is like a foreign language to the beginning CBer, this dictionary and cross-reference is intended to provide a quick and easy guide for learning CB slanguage.

Since CB slanguage does vary greatly from section to section of the country, and because it continues to expand rapidly (keeping pace with today's CB boom), I hope that this book will be a 'must' to the long time CBer who wishes to be knowledgeable in CB terminology currently used throughout the nation. Additionally, THE 'OFFICIAL' CB SLANGUAGE LANGUAGE DICTIONARY AND CROSS-REFERENCE will prove invaluable to those who do not actively talk on the CB, but who monitor or are simply interested in acquiring an understanding of CB's fascinating and colorful lingo.

The pages of this dictionary and cross-reference contain terminology from every section of the country. Thousands of travelled miles and thousands of monitored conversations, both base and mobile, have produced the bulk of the material. Much of the balance was obtained from interviews with CBers, and from terms sent to me by CBers across the country.

Compiling the book was at once interesting hard work and continuously exciting fun. I hope that the reader will find the dictionary and cross-reference amusing as well as a useful tool for learning and interpreting CB slanguage.

The slanguage of CB is steadily growing and new terms are born daily. If you have a new term which you would like to see included in a subsequent revision of this work, please fill in and return the form located on page 245.

To all those who have already sent terms to me, I am extremely grateful. "We be putting the good numbers on you and yours."

—Lanie Dills.

BEGINNERS' GUIDE TO TRANSMISSION

Initially, most beginners are afraid to talk on the CB because they are unfamiliar with CB slanguage. They are usually somewhat embarrassed by their first efforts and they suffer from a condition commonly known as "mike fright." The information provided below should serve as a helpful guide for new CBers in their first difficult stages.

I. INITIAL TRANSMISSIONS

The first thing to remember when making a transmission is that you must, according to FCC Rules, identify yourself by your callsign. Your callsign is a combination of letters and numbers assigned to you by the FCC with your CB License. As of April 16, 1976, the FCC has made provision for new CBers to use a temporary callsign for 60 days after applying for an official CB Station License (see Temporary Permit System, page vii.)

In addition to your callsign, you may wish to use frequent CB terms, such as "break," "breaker, broke," or "break 10" (or other channel number). Also, you may choose to identify yourself by your handle, your CB code name.

Sample: "Break 10. This is KXL-5375, the Nashville Popsicle."

You may have a number of purposes for breaking into the channel. Below we have listed some of the most frequent ones and the common terms to signify them.

A. <u>To call a specific person</u>:
   COLLECT CALL
   BREAK FOR (*individual's callsign and handle*)
   LONG DISTANCE TELEPHONE IS RINGING FOR (*individual's callsign and handle*)
   Sample: "This is KXL-5375, the Nashville Popsicle; I have a collect call for that Sugar Britches."

B. <u>To transmit emergency information</u> (transmission should be made on Channel 9, the channel officially designated and monitored for emergency messages:
   10-34 ('Official' 10-Code number to indicate emergency)
   10-33 (Abbreviated 10-Code number)
   Sample: "Break Channel 9. We've got a 10-34 on 140 at Exit 215."

C. <u>To obtain police location and road condition reports</u>:
   BEAR STORY
   FIX
   LEFT SHOULDER
   SMOKEY REPORT
   Sample: "Breaker, KXI-7248, Sugar Britches here, looking for a westbound 18-wheeler. How does it look over your left shoulder?"

D. <u>To obtain directions</u>:
   Give your location (what the CBers call your *twenty*) and the location desired.
   Sample: "Break 10. This is KXI-7248, the Sugar Britches. I'm at Interstate 40, exit 215. How do I get to White's Creek Road?"

E. <u>To obtain a radio check</u>:
   METER READING
   COPY
   POUNDS ("S" units on meter)
   10-32
   Sample: "Break 10 for a radio check. This is KXI-7248. How many pounds am I putting on you?"

F. <u>To obtain correct time</u>:
   10-34 (Abbreviated 10-Code)
   10-36 ('Official' 10-Code)
   Sample: "KXI-7248. The Sugar Britches here, breaking for a 10-36."

II. SEEKING RESPONSES

Several terms indicate that you wish someone to respond to you. Perhaps the most common are:
   COME BACK
   COME ON
   GO AHEAD
   GO BREAKER
   WE'RE LISTENING
   Sample: "KXL-5375, the Nashville Popsicle here. Come back on that radio check."

III. SIGN-OFF

As in the initial transmission, you must sign off with your callsign. But in addition, you may wish to indicate that you will either be listening or leaving the air entirely.

A. <u>Through talking but monitoring</u>:
   COPYING THE MAIL
   DOWN AND ON THE SIDE
   EARS ON
   LAY OVER AND LISTEN
   ON STANDBY
   10-10
   Sample: "The one Nashville Popsicle, KXL-5375. We're down and on the side."

B. <u>Through talking and leaving the air</u>:
   ADIOS
   CLEAR
   CUT LOOSE
   GONE
   OUT
   Sample: "KXL-5375, we're clear."

IV. DURATION OF TRANSMISSION

Under FCC regulations, CB transmissions are limited to no more than 5 consecutive minutes, with a break of at least one minute before resuming transmission.

TEMPORARY PERMIT SYSTEM

After filing an application with the FCC for an official CB Station License (Form 505), you are eligible for a temporary CB Permit which is valid for 60 days from the day you file your Official Station License application.

For your Temporary Permit, fill out FCC Form 555B (it is available at most retail CB outlets and at all offices of the Federal Communications Commission). Keep the completed Form 555B and use your temporary callsign—which consists of the letter "K" followed by the first letter of your first name, the first letter of your last name and your zip code—until your Station License arrives.

If you have not received your Station License within the 60-day Temporary Permit period, contact the Public Reference Section, Amateur and Citizens Division, Federal Communications Commission, Washington, D.C. 20554, phone number (202) 632-7175. Give the FCC your name and address as it appeared on your application. If you've moved since applying for your license, state that fact in your letter and be sure to give your new address.

BEGINNERS' GUIDE TO TRANSMISSION IN CANADA

The Canadian Department of Communications (DOC) oversees the General Radio Service (GRS)—the civilian two-way radio system of Canada. The GRS operates on Channels 1 through 22 (expected to be expanded to 40 channels eventually). Channel 9 is designated by the DOC as the Emergency Channel.

A GRS operator must obtain a General Radio Service License from the DOC. The DOC assigns a callsign with each GRS License issued. Under DOC regulations, a GRS operator must identify himself or herself by this callsign at the beginning and end of each transmission. In addition, DOC regulations limit the length of transmission to five consecutive minutes, with a two-minute break before resuming transmission.

For complete information, you may obtain a copy of "The General Radio Service License Handbook" for 75¢ from Printing and Publishing Supply and Services, Department of Communications, Government of Canada, Ottawa, Ontario, K1A 0S9, Canada. Request Catalog Item #C023-5-1975.

US/CANADIAN RECIPROCAL OPERATING AGREEMENT

If you are a CBer with a valid Class D License or Temporary Permit issued by the FCC, you are eligible for a Registration Permit (free-of-charge) from the Department of Communications of the Canadian Government. It will allow you to operate your station in Canada.

To apply, you need a copy of your Class D License or Temporary Permit issued by the FCC, and an application form (Form #1652) available from any of the five Canadian Department of Communications branch offices. It is suggested that you contact the Office of Regional Director, Telecommunications Regulation, Communications Canada, at the DOC branch office nearest to your area of proposed station operation to obtain the necessary forms. The DOC branch offices are located in Vancouver, British Columbia; Winnepeg, Manitoba; Toronto, Ontario; Montreal, Quebec; and Mancton, New Brunswick.

You can apply for your Canadian Registration Permit by mail at least 6 weeks in advance of your trip to Canada. Or, upon arriving in Canada, you can go to the nearest DOC office with your valid FCC Class D License or Temporary Permit, apply in person and receive your Registration Permit immediately. If you apply by mail, be sure to attach a copy of your FCC Class D license or Temporary Permit.

Upon obtaining your Canadian Registration Permit, you will be bound to operate your station under the DOC regulations for the General Radio Service. You must also always have your valid FCC Class D License or Temporary Permit on your person when operating your station. You will still use your FCC-assigned callsign to identify yourself at the beginning and end of each transmission.

Your Canadian Registration Permit is valid until the expiration date of your FCC Class D License or Temporary Permit.

CANADIAN/US RECIPROCAL OPERATING AGREEMENT

If you are a licensed GRS operator with a valid General Radio Service License issued by the Canadian Department of Communications, you are eligible for an FCC Operating Permit (free-of-charge) which will allow you to operate your station in the United States.

You may obtain an application form for an Operating Permit (FCC Form 410-B) from the Federal Communications Commission, Gettysburg, Pennsylvania, U.S.A. 17325. After filling out the form and returning it to the FCC in Gettysburg, you will receive your FCC Operating Permit by mail in approximately four weeks.

It is possible to apply in person at any office of the FCC for an Operating Permit; however, there will still be a four-week delay since all applications must be processed through Gettysburg, Pennsylvania.

As a GRS operator in the U.S., you must always have your Canadian GRS License on your person when transmitting. You must also identify yourself at the beginning and end of each transmission or series of transmissions with the callsign assigned to you by the Canadian DOC and the location (city and state) of your transmission. GRS operators transmitting in the U.S. under an FCC Operating Permit must operate their stations in accordance with Part 95 of FCC Rules and Regulations.

An FCC Operating Permit is valid for one year from the date of issue or until the expiration date of the holder's GRS License, whichever comes first.

Dictionary

KEY: MW - midwest U.S.
   NE - northeast U.S.
   NW - northwest U.S.
    S - south U.S.
   SE - southeast U.S.
   SW - southwest U.S.
    W - west U.S.

A-F: audio frequency.

A-M: amplitude modulation, a technique of varying the power output so it can be used for conveying messages.

A-N-L: automatic noise limiter (a device in most CB rigs to reduce ignition noise interference).

ABSITIVELY AND POSILUTELY: definite agreement (NE).

ACE: friend.

ACT OF MENTAL GRATIFICATION: flattering; stroking (NE).

ADIOS: sign-off; finished talking (SW).

ADVERTISING: a marked police car with its lights turned on.

AFFIRMATIVE: yes.

AFTER BURNER: linear amplifier.

AIR BEAR: police in helicopter.

AIR CAP 8: Wichita, Kansas.

AIR JOCKEY: pilot.

ALAMO CITY (or TOWN): San Antonio, Texas (SW).

ALERT: Affiliated League of Emergency Radio Teams, Suite 818A, National Press Building, Washington, D.C. 20004.

ALICE IN WONDERLAND: driver who appears lost or confused about where he's turning.

ALL CLEAN: vehicle(s) on the road or parked are not police; no police around; e.g. "It's all clean on this rip strip."

ALL WASHED OUT: vehicles(s) on road or parked are not police; e.g. "You got a 4-wheeler on the westbound side at milepost 112. It be all washed out."

ALLIGATOR: CBer who talks too much; CBer who has a "big mouth."

ALLIGATOR STATION: CBer who talks too much and doesn't listen; CB radio that transmits but does not receive.

ANCHOR IT: brake quickly for emergency stop.

ANCHORED MODULATOR: base or field station CB operator.

ANGEL CITY: Los Angeles, California.

ANKLEBITER: very young child; unruly child; child (NE).

ANTENNA FARM: base station with a number of large antennas.

APPLE: CBer who operates illegally; constant, old-time CBer.

APPLE CITY (or CAPITAL): Winchester, Virginia (SE)

APPLIANCE OPERATOR: CBer who is ignorant about his radio.

ARKANSAS CREDIT CARD: rubber siphon hose (SW).

ARMCHAIR COPY: sending out a very strong signal.

ART CART: van brightly painted with creative design.

ASTRO TOWN: Houston, Texas.

ASTRODOME CITY: Houston, Texas (SE).

ATTILLA THE HUN: bad mechanic.

AVIATOR: speeding driver; e.g. "That aviator is looking to feed the bears."

B TOWN: Birmingham, Alabama (SE).

B-A-R TEAM: tough group of truckers.

B.G. TOWN: Bowling Green, Kentucky.

B.R. TOWN: Baton Rouge, Louisiana.

B-T-O: experienced CBer (abbreviation for big time operator) (NE).

B.W.: Baltimore, Maryland.

BABY BEAR: rookie policeman.

BACK: over; back to you; answer back.

BACK AT 'CHA: answering back; e.g. "You got the one Night Stalker back at 'cha!"

BACK AT YOU: answer back.

BACK DOOR: last CB vehicle in a group of two or more.

BACK DOOR CLOSED: rear CB vehicle in a line of two or more watching for police.

BACK DOOR SEALED UP: rear CBer will notify others if police are on the move from behind.

BACK DOOR SHUT: last CB vehicle watching behind for police or speeding vehicles.

BACK DOWN: slow down.

BACK 'EM OFF: slow down.

BACK 'EM ON DOWN or UP: stop transmitting; slow down (SE).

BACK 'EM UP: slow down; stop transmitting (SE).

BACK IN A SHORT, SHORT: CBer will return to the channel shortly.

BACK IT ON OUT: stop transmitting.

BACK OFF: stop transmitting; slow down.

BACK OFF ON IT: slow down (SE).

BACK OFF THE HAMMER: slow down (SE).

BACK ON DOWN: stop transmitting; slow down (SE).

BACK OUT: stop transmitting.

BACK OUT OF IT: stop transmitting; slow down.

BACK SEAT: CBer monitoring the set; e.g. "Let the channel roll; we've got the Sugar Britches in the back seat."

BACK TO YOU: answering back; e.g. "You've got the Sugar Britches back to you."

BACKGROUND: noise preventing clear transmission.

BACKGROUND TOO HEAVY: background noise too strong (SE)

BACKSLIDE: return trip (SE); e.g. "Definitely did enjoy the rachet jawing; we'll catch you on the backslide."

BACKSTROKE: return trip (SE).

BACKYARD: the road behind; e.g. "Take a look in your backyard, good buddy, and give me a bear report."

BAD SCENE: overcrowded CB channel.

BAGGING THEM: police catching speeders (NE).

BAL CITY: Baltimore, Maryland.

BALLET DANCER: antenna swaying in the wind (NE).

BALLOON FREIGHT: lightweight freight.

BALLOON TIRES: radial tires.

BALONEYS: tires.

BAMBI: innocent or naive motorist or other person.

BANANA PEEL: yellow stripe down the middle of the road.

BAND-AID: ambulance (NE).

BANG A U-EY: make a U-turn (NE).

BANG 'EM UP: traffic accident.

BAR CITY: Forrest City, Arkansas (SE).

BAREBACK: running without a CB radio (SW).

BAREBACK TRACTOR: tractor cab without trailer.

BAREFOOT: legal operation of CB in terms of power; e.g. "Hey, good buddy, are you sure you're running barefoot in that mobile? You're blowing my windows out."

BAREFOOT MOBILE: mobile CB rig with no extra power.

BARLEY POP: beer (NW)

BARN: truck garage.

BARNIE: state trooper (SW).

BARNYARD: trailer hauling livestock.

BARYPHONY: speech difficulty.

BASE RADIO: CB set installed in home or other immovable location.

BASE RIG: CB set installed in home or other immovable location.

BASE STATION: transceiver installed at a fixed location and primarily used for communicating with mobile units and other base stations.

BASEBALL CITY: Youngstown, Ohio.

BASEBALL RADIO: AM car radio (MW).

BASEMENT: Channel 1 (NW) e.g. "Too many rachet jawers on this channel, let's go to the basement."

BASKETBALL ON CHANNEL #9 (*or other channel*): monitoring Channel #9 (or other channel).

BAY CITY: San Francisco, California (W).

BEACH BALL BUGGY: Gremlin automobile (SW).

BEACH CITY: Fort Lauderdale, Florida.

BEAM: a type of antenna which is highly directional.

BEAN HAULER: trucker hauling fruits and vegetables.

BEAN STORE: restaurant.

BEAN TOWN: Boston, Massachusetts (NE).

BEAN WAGON: coffee wagon.

BEAR: police of any kind.

BEAR BAIT: speeding car without CB (SE); e.g. "Here comes some bear bait 'round ya, let them feed the bears at Exit 84."

BEAR BAIT PASSENGER: car without CB which will speed past and be caught by police (SE).

BEAR BITE: speeding ticket (SE).

BEAR BUSTER: a CB converter which is installed on an AM car radio and permits monitoring of CB conversation.

BEAR CAGE: police station.

BEAR CAVE: police or highway patrol station (W).

BEAR FOOD: speeding vehicle without CB.

BEAR HUG: police using handcuffs or other restraints; physical abuse by police.

BEAR IN THE AIR: police helicopter.

BEAR IN THE SKY: police helicopter.

BEAR MAKING LIKE BUCK ROGERS: police with a radar gun (SW); e.g. "We got a bear making like Buck Rogers at this milepost 190."

BEAR MEAT: speeding car without CB.

BEAR REPORT: police location report; e.g. "How about an eastbound 18-wheeler, we need a bear report, good buddy."

BEAR SITUATION: police location report.

BEAR STORY: police location report (SE); e.g. "How about that eastbound side? Tell me a bear story."

BEAR TAKING PICTURES: police with radar.

BEAR TRAP: radar set-up; e.g. "There's a bear trap at Exit 85."

BEARDED BUDDY: police of any kind (SE).

BEARS ARE CRAWLING: police or troopers are switching from side to side of the expressway (SE); state police with radar.

BEARS' DEN: police station.

BEARS' LAIR: police station.

BEARS WALL-TO-WALL: police are everywhere; radar set-up or road block.

BEAST: CB rig; CB in the repair shop (NE).

BEAT THE BUSHES: the "front door" (lead CB vehicle) looks for police and warns CBers behind him of police location.

BEAVER: woman or girl.

BEAVER CLEAVER: truck driver who has a way with women.

BEAVER HUNT: looking for women.

BEAVER PATROL: looking for women.

BEAVER WITH A KICK STAND: long-haired male (SW).

BEDBUG: Volkswagen camper (NE).

BEDBUG HAULER: moving van.

BEEF CITY: Kansas City, Missouri.

BEER CITY: Milwaukee, Wisconsin (MW).

BEING EAST (*or NORTH, SOUTH, WEST*): driving east (or *north, south, west*).

BELLY UP: turned-over vehicle.

BENCH: CBer monitoring the set; e.g. "I don't know the twenty, but maybe someone on the bench does."

BENDING THE WINDOWS: clear reception of signal (SE).

BENNY CHASER: strong coffee.

BETTER COOL IT: slow down.

BETTER HALF: wife; husband; other person in conversation who isn't transmitting (MW).

BICENTENNIAL CITY: Philadelphia, Pennsylvania (NE).

BIG A: Amarillo, Texas (SW); Atlanta, Georgia (SE).

BIG APPLE (THE): New York City (NE).

BIG ARCH: St. Louis, Missouri.

BIG B: Birmingham, Alabama (SE).

BIG BLUE-EYED INDIAN: Navajo truck (MW).

BIG BROTHER: police of any kind; Philadelphia, Pennsylvania.

BIG BUTTE: Butte, Montana.

BIG C: Chicago, Illinois.

BIG CAR: tractor trailer truck.

BIG D; BIG D CITY (or TOWN):   Dallas, Texas (SW); Denver, Colorado; Des Moines, Iowa.

BIG DADDY: FCC.

BIG DOG: Greyhound bus.

BIG DUMMY: affectionate term for truck driver; friend.

BIG E: Erie, Pennsylvania.

BIG EARS: clear reception of signal.

BIG EIGHTS: sign-off; best wishes.

BIG HAT: state trooper.

BIG LADY: New York City.

BIG M: Memphis, Tennessee (SE); Miami, Florida.

BIG MAMA: 9-foot whip antenna.

BIG OAK: Oakland, California.

BIG ORANGE: Snyder truck.

BIG PORT: Portland, Oregon.

BIG R: truck belonging to Roadway Freight System (SE); e.g. "How about ya, Big R. Got your ears on?"

BIG RIG: tractor trailer truck.

BIG SALTY: Salt Lake City, Utah.

BIG SKIP LANE: heaven.

BIG SKY: Billings, Montana.

BIG SLAB: expressway (SE).

BIG SOUTH (THE):   Atlanta, Georgia.

BIG T: Tampa, Florida; Tucson, Arizona (SW).

BIG TEN-FOUR (A):   10-4 emphatically; definitely
    yes; okay; I'll go along with that; e.g. "A big 10-4 on
    that smokey report, good buddy."

BIG THREES: sign-off; best wishes.

BIG TWIN: Minneapolis, Minnesota.

BIKINI STATE: Florida.

BINDERS: brakes.

BIRD: Ford Thunderbird.

BIRD-DOGGIN':   following closely behind another
    vehicle (so police radar will catch only the first
    vehicle).

BIRD IN THE AIR: police helicopter (SE).

BIRDYBACK: tractor trailer carrying freight con-
    tainer to or from aircraft.

BISCUITS AND GRAVY: food.

BIT BY THE BEAR: given a speeding ticket by the
    police.

BIT ON THE SEAT OF THE BRITCHES: got a
    speeding ticket (SE)

BLACK AND WHITE: police car; police.

BLACK AND WHITE CBer: police car with CB (W).

BLACK BOX: linear amplifier.

BLACK WATER: coffee (SE).

BLEED OVER: transmission from one channel
    runs over into another; interference.

BLEEDING: signal too strong, switch channels (NW); background interrupting transmission (SE).

BLESSED EVENT: new CB radio (NW).

BLEW MY DOORS OFF: passed me with great speed; e.g. "The Texas Road Runner just blew my doors off."

BLIND: area of road not visible to driver.

BLIND SIDE: passenger (right) side of vehicle.

BLINKIN' WINKIN': school bus.

BLOCK: to send out a signal so strong it interferes with other channels.

BLOCKING THE CHANNEL: keying the mike to prevent messages (SE).

BLOOD BOX: ambulance.

BLOW THE DOORS OFF: pass another vehicle.

BLOWING SMOKE: reception coming in clear and strong.

BLOWING YOUR DOORS IN: passing your vehicle; e.g. "Back on down, I'll be blowing your doors in on the fifty dollar lane."

BLOWN PUMPKIN: tire blow-out.

BLUE AND WHITE: police (MW).

BLUE BOYS: local police (SE, SW).

BLUE GRASS STATE: Kentucky.

BLUE JEANS: state troopers (MW).

BLUE LIGHT: marked police car.

BLUE SLIP: speeding ticket (SW).

BOARDWALK (THE):   Atlantic City, New Jersey.

BOAST TOASTIE: experienced CBer (NW).

BOBTAIL: tractor without trailer.

BOB-TAILING: vehicle without CB following one so equipped.

BODACIOUS: clear reception of signal (SE); e.g. "Mercy sakes, Snow Flake, you're just sounding bodacious out there tonight."

BOGEY: two or more axles.

BOLL WEEVIL: inexperienced truck driver.

BOMB: very strong signal; e.g. "You're puttin' a bomb in here; you got boots on?"

BONE BOX: ambulance.

BONEYARD: cemetery; place for junk vehicles.

BOOB TUBE: television.

BOOGIE FEVER: slow-moving vehicle (SE).

BOOGIE MAN: state trooper (NW).

BOOGIEING: nightclubbing.

BOOM IT DOWN: tighten the chains holding down cargo.

BOOM WAGON: truck hauling dangerous cargo.

BOOMERS: binders on a flatbed trailer for tightening chains around cargo.

BOONDOCK: avoid weigh stations by taking back roads at night.

BOONDOCKS: anyplace that's out-of-the-way from any city; sparsely populated area.

BOONIES: place far from a city and people (the boondocks).

BOOT 'ER OVER: let another CBer transmit; e.g. "Hey good buddy, boot 'er over and give that Triple M a break one time."

BOOT JOCKEY: pedestrian on road.

BOOT REST: accelerator pedal.

BOOTLEG: transmit without a license.

BOOTLEGGER: unlicensed CBer; CBer who uses false call sign.

BOOTLEGGING: using another's CB (W).

BOOTS: linear amplifier to boost CB output.

BOOTS ON: using linear amplifier (MW)

BORDER TOWN: El Paso, Texas.

BOTH FEET ON THE FLOOR: vehicle is moving at fastest possible rate of speed.

BOTTLE POPPER: beverage truck.

BOULEVARD: expressway (SE); highway.

BOULEVARD OF BROKEN DREAMS: road with a great many speed traps.

BOUNCE-AROUND: return trip (SE); e.g. "See you on the bounce-around, good buddy."

BOUNCING CARDBOARD: driver's license.

BOW OUT: to sign off and stop transmitting.

BOX: tractor trailer truck, square and enclosed (SE); CB set (SE); camper.

BOX ON WHEELS: hearse.

BOY SCOUTS: state police (NE).

BOZOS: late night CBers in Nashville, Tennessee (SE).

BRANCH BANK: armored truck.

BRASS: important person, usually an executive or official.

BREAD: money.

BREAK or BREAK, BREAK: request for use of a channel; any attempt to break into a transmission.

BREAK CHANNEL (*number*):   breaking into the channel.

BREAK FOR (*handle*):   call for a specific CBer; e.g. "Break for that Cactus Jack just one time."

BREAK 10 (*or other channel #*):   requesting permission to speak on Channel 10 (or other channel indicated).

BREAK THE OLD NEEDLE: clear reception of signal (SE).

BREAK THE UNIT: uncouple tractor from trailer.

BREAKER (*direction*)BOUND 18:   breaking into a channel to talk with any 18-wheeler going in a certain direction; e.g. "breaker westbound 18"; also, request for police location and road condition report.

BREAKER BROKE: request to use a channel; attempt to break into a transmission.

BREAKER BUSTED: used when someone has been breaking and requesting to speak on channel without getting anywhere (NE).

BREAKING UP: signal is not coming in constantly; signal coming intermittently.

BREAKING WIND: first CB vehicle in a line of two or more watches for police, obstructions (MW).

BREEZE IT: disregard what I said.

BREW: beer.

BRICK: a small hand-held transceiver.

BRING IT BACK: answer back (SE).

BRING IT ON: answer back; come up here where I am; the way is clear.

BRING IT UP: move your vehicle up closer.

BRING ON YOUR MACHINE: come this way; bring your vehicle up here.

BRING YOURSELF ON IN: move into the right lane (SE); answer back (SE).

BROUGHT IT ON: come on up here; the way is clear; answer back.

BROUGHT YOURSELF ON IN (or UP): move up.

BRUISING MY BODY: interrupting my transmission.

BROWN BOTTLE: beer.

BROWN COW: New Jersey.

BROWN PAPER BAG: unmarked police car (NE).

BROWNIE: auxiliary transmission.

BRUSH YOUR TEETH AND COMB YOUR HAIR: police radar ahead, slow down to avoid getting caught by radar unit (NW).

BUBBLE MACHINE: vehicle with flashing lights; police.

BUBBLE TROUBLE: tire ailments.

BUBBLEGUM MACHINE: vehicle with flashing lights, usually police car.

BUBBLEGUMMER: teenage CBer (W); teenager.

BUCKET MOUTH: loud mouth or gossip; obscene or profane talker.

BUCKET OF BOLTS: tractor trailer rig (MW).

BUCKEYE STATE: Ohio.

BUCKSHOT: interference coming from another channel, which comes through unintelligibly.

BUDDY: fellow trucker (SE).

BUDWEISER CITY: St. Louis, Missouri.

BUFFALO: man; husband.

BUFFER (THE): Buffalo, New York.

BUG OUT: leave the channel.

BUGGERHOLE BUNCH: Irvine, California (W).

BUGS ON THE GLASS: insects on the windshield.

BULL JOCKEY: idle talker, one who uses his CB rig to pass the time of day.

BULL RACK: truck hauling animals (NW).

BULLDOG: Mack truck.

BULLET LANE: passing lane (SE); e.g. "Who we got in that Thunder Chicken in the bullet lane?"

BULLS: police.

BUMBLE BEE: two-cycle engine.

BUMPER JUMPER: vehicle following too closely; tailgating vehicle.

BUMPER LANE: passing lane.

BURNING PAINT: vehicle on fire (MW).

BURNING UP MY EARS: strong signal coming in.

BURRITO CITY: El Paso, Texas.

BUSCH CITY: St. Louis, Missouri.

BUSHEL: 1,000 pounds (half a ton).

BUSHEL BASKET: unit for storage of freight; trailer of an 18-wheeler.

BUSTED SIDEWALK: detour (MW).

BUSTED ZIPPER: unlocked or open rear door.

BUTTERMILK: beer (SE).

BUTTONPUSHER: one who keys his microphone without speaking, which causes computer interference and humming noise; also prevents messages.

BUTTONPUSHING: keying the mike without speaking (prevents messages).

BUYING AN ORCHARD: gazing off the road into the trees.

CB: Citizens Band radio.

CB LAND: network of CBers.

CQ: calling any station.

CRW: Community Radio Watch.

C-W: stands for Morse Code (C-W is an abbreviation for continuous wave).

CAB: portion of truck where driver sits.

CABBIE: taxicab driver.

CACKLE CRATE: truck hauling live poultry.

CACTUS JUICE: liquor (SW).

CACTUS PATCH: Phoenix, Arizona; Roswell, New Mexico (SW).

CALLING FOR: asking for; e.g. "I'm calling for that Cactus Jack, do you copy?"

CALLSIGN: official FCC assignment of letters and numbers to a CB operator.

CAMERA: police radar; e.g. "There's a smokey with a camera at milepost 108."

CAMERA CAR: police vehicle with radar.

CAMPER: mobile massage parlor (NE).

CANDY MAN: FCC.

CANDY STORE: lively truckers' hangout.

CAPITAL J: Jackson, Mississippi (SE).

CARPET CRAWLER: child (SW).

CARRIER: person who keys the mike but doesn't transmit (NE).

CARRIER THROWER: CBer who keys the mike without talking; CBer who jams the channel (MW).

CARTEL: group of CBers hogging the channel (NW).

CASA: home (SW).

CASH REGISTER: toll booth.

CATBOX: restroom.

CATCH: talk to; e.g. "Catch you on the flip-flop."

CATCH CAR: police car beyond radar set-up.

CATCH YOU COME LATER: talk to you again; speak to you at a later time (SW).

CATCH YOU ON THE FLIPPER: catch you on the radio on the return trip.

CATCH YOU ON THE OLD FLIP-FLOP: catch you on the radio on a return trip.

CATCH YOU ON THE REVERSE: speak to you on the CB on the return trip.

CATCHA' LATER: sign-off (MW).

CATS AND DOGS: heavy rain (MW).

CATTLE STATE: Kansas.

CATTLE TOWN: Chicago, Illinois.

CEMENT MIXER: truck with a noisy transmission or engine.

CHAIN GANG: CB club members (NW).

CHAIR CITY: Grand Rapids, Michigan.

CHANNEL CLOWN HOG: channel hog (MW).

CHANNEL CONTROL: person who directs traffic on the channel.

CHANNEL HOGGER: CBer who talks too long.

CHANNEL 9:   emergency channel.

CHANNEL 10:   channel most truckers east of Kansas City have used in the past.

CHANNEL 19:   channel truckers use.

CHANNEL 25:   telephone (NE).

CHAPTER 13:   New York City.

CHARLEY: FCC.

CHARLIE: Charleston, South Carolina.

CHARLIE (or CHARLIE, CHARLIE):   yes.

CHARLIE BROWN: yes.

CHARLIE TOWN: Lake Charles, Louisiana (SW).

CHASE CAR: police car guided by a concealed radar unit.

CHASER: police car beyond radar who catches speeders.

CHECK THE SEAT COVERS: look at the passengers, usually women.

CHECKING MY EYELIDS FOR PIN HOLES: tired, sleepy (W).

CHERRY PICKER: high truck cab.

CHEW AND CHOKE: restaurant.

CHEW THE FAT: talk idly on the CB; gossip.

CHI TOWN: Chicago, Illinois.

CHICK: woman; girl (NE).

CHICKEN BOX: CB radio.

CHICKEN CHOKER: one who masturbates; poultry truck; friendly term truckers use for each other; overweight load; D-104 type microphone user (NE).

CHICKEN COOP: weigh station; e.g. "The chicken coop is clean, bring it on up here."

CHICKEN COOP IS CLEAN: weigh station is closed.

CHICKEN INSPECTOR: weigh station inspector.

CHICKEN SNATCHER: thief (MW).

CHIEF HOOD LIFTER: garage superintendent.

CHIT CHAT: make small talk.

CHOKE THE CHICKEN: masturbate.

CHOKING A CHICKEN: using the restroom (MW); using a D-104 microphone (NE).

CHOO-CHOO TOWN: Chattanooga, Tennessee (SE).

CHOO-CHOO TRAIN: tractor pulling two trailers.

CHOPPED TOP: short antenna (NE).

CHOPPER: helicopter.

CHOPPER IN THE AIR: police helicopter.

CHOPTOP: short antenna.

CHOWDOWN: eat (usually a large meal).

CHRISTMAS CARD: speeding ticket (NE).

CHROME DOME: roof-mounted antenna.

CIGAR CITY: Tampa, Florida.

CINCY: Cincinnati, Ohio.

CINDERELLA WORLD: Disneyland, California (W).

CIRCLE CITY: Indianapolis, Indiana (MW).

CIRCUS CITY: Sarasota, Florida.

CITY FLYER: truck with a short, low trailer, used for making city deliveries.

CITY KITTY: local police (MW).

CITY OF ROSES: Portland, Oregon.

CLASS A STATION: a CB service station licensed to operate from 460 to 470 MHz in the UHF band.

CLASS C STATION: radio station authorized to transmit controlled signals on specified frequencies in the 26.96 to 27.26 MHz and 72 to 76 MHz bands.

CLASS D STATION: a CB service station licensed to use radio telephony on authorized channels in the 26.96 to 27.26 MHz band. Most CBers have Class D stations.

CLEAN: no police or obstructions.

CLEAN AND GREEN: road clear of police and obstructions (SW).

CLEAN AS A HOUND'S TOOTH: road is clear of police and obstructions (SE).

CLEAN CUT: unmodified CB radio set (NW).

CLEAN SHOT: road is clear of police and obstructions (SE).

CLEAN UP: to be sexually promiscuous (MW); e.g. "I went to Chi Town to clean up, but I ended up choking my chicken."

CLEANER CHANNEL: channel with less interference.

CLEAR: sign-off; through transmitting.

CLEAR AFTER YOU: after you sign off, the channel will be clear.

CLEAR AND ROLLING: sign-off and moving (SE).

CLEAR AS A SPRING DAY: road is clear of police and obstructions (SE).

CLEAR SHOT: road clear of police and obstructions.

CLEAR THERE WITH YOU: sign-off; through transmitting (SE).

CLEARING THE WAY: first CB vehicle in a line of two or more watches for police, obstructions.

CLOSE-TALK: speak with the mike held close to the mouth.

CLOSE THE GATES: close the rear doors of a tractor trailer.

CLOTHESLINE: mobile telephone (MW); telephone or power lines crossing low over the roadway.

CO-AX: coaxial cable.

COCKLEBURR: pep pill (SE).

COFFEE POT: restaurant.

COFFEEBREAK: small gathering of CBers.

COFFIN: sleeper box of truck tractor (NE).

COFFIN BOX: sleeping area separate from truck cab.

COKE STOP: restroom stop (SW).

COLD COFFEE: beer (SE).

COLLECT CALL: call for a specific CBer.

COLORADO KOOL AID: beer (SW).

COLORS GOING UP: lights on police vehicle beginning to flash.

COME AGAIN: repeat message.

COME BACK: answer back once more; e.g. "One more come back, Sugar Britches, and then we cut loose."

COME HERE: answer back.

COME ON: answer back; e.g. "You got the Shotgun, come on."

COME ON BACK: repeat your message.

COME ON BREAKER: CBer breaking in should begin talking.

COMIC BOOKS: trucker's log sheets or log books; pornography.

COMING IN LOUD AND PROUD: clear reception of signal (SE).

COMING IN TOO TORRIBLE: signal too strong (SE).

COMING OUT OF THE WINDOWS: clear reception of signal (SE).

CONCENTRATOR: driver.

CONCRETE JUNGLE: expressway (W).

CONFAB: get-together to discuss something important.

CONFETTI: snow.

CONVAC: conversation (SE).

CONVOY: a procession of CB vehicles traveling the expressway together, and keeping in constant touch via CB.

COOKIES: cigarettes.

COOKING: driving (SE, MW).

COOKING GOOD: acquired desired speed (MW).

COPY: message; do you understand?; e.g. "Anybody copy this lil' ol' mobile?"

COPYING THE MAIL: listening; monitoring the CB.

CORN BINDER: International Truck (NW).

CORN CELLAR: liquor store.

CORN FLAKE: Consolidated Freightway truck.

CORN SQUEEZINGS: liquor (NE).

CORN SYRUP: liquor (NE).

COTTONPICKER: friendly term truckers use for each other.

COUNTRY CADILLAC: tractor trailer truck (SE).

COUNTRY JOE: rural police (MW).

COUNTY MOUNTY: Sheriff's Department (SE).

COUNTY MOUNTY BOUNTY: fine levied on a driver; particularly in a situation where he must pay up or spend the night in jail, without benefit of a hearing or trial.

COUPON: speeding ticket (SE); e.g. "Mercy sakes, I've already got enough coupons to paper my wall."

COUSIN CHARLEY: FCC.

COVER: woman; girl (NE).

COVER GROUND: speed up.

COVERED UP: too much interference; I can't understand you; signal isn't clear.

COW SQUEEZINGS: milk (NE).

COW TOWN: Ft. Worth, Texas (SE, SW).

COWBOY: unsafe or reckless driver.

COWBOY CADILLAC: pick-up truck (MW); El Camino or Ford Ranchero.

COWBOY TRUCKER: trucker whose rig has lots of chrome.

CRACKER BOX: very small car; Volkswagen van (SW).

CRADLE BABY: CBer who breaks in but seems afraid or nervous about speaking (NE).

CREAM PUFF: short freight haul.

CREEPER GEAR: lowest gear, or combination of gears, to get extra power.

CROCODILE STATION: CB station that monitors but doesn't transmit (MW).

CROSSING THE HUMP: going over a mountain (SE).

CRUMB CRUSHERS: children (SE).

CRYSTAL: a piece of quartz whose physical dimensions determine the frequency at which it will function as a resonant circuit.

CUB SCOUTS: sheriff's assistants (NW).

'CUDA: Plymouth Barracuda.

CUP OF MUD: coffee.

CUT LOOSE: sign-off; stop transmitting (SE).

CUT OUT: leave the channel (NW).

CUT SOME Z's: get some sleep.

CUT THE CO-AX: turn off the CB set.

D-B: power ratio.

D.C.:   Washington, D. C.

D.O.C.:   Canada's Department of Communications, equivalent of FCC.

D.O.T.:   truck weigh or inspection station (abbreviation for Department of Transportation).

D.O.T. MAN: Department of Transportation representative who stops trucks to check lights, overloads, log books, etc., and gives tickets for violations.

D-X: long distance.

DADDY-O: FCC (NW).

DAGO: San Diego, California.

DANDRUFF: light snow.

DANIEL BOONE TIME: hunting season.

DARK TIME: night (NW).

DEAD CITY: Erie, Pennsylvania.

DEAD FOOT: driver going below posted speed limit.

DEAD HEAD: returning home quickly, without stopping.

DEAD HEADING: driving with an empty truck or trailer; driving empty on gas.

DEAD PEDAL: slow-moving vehicle.

DEAD SPOT: disappearance of signal, caused by local geographic conditions.

DECIBEL (DB): a unit for expression of the ratio of two values, usually power or voltage. It is most often used by CBers in reference to the coaxial cable attenuation loss of antenna gain.

DECOY: unmanned police car.

DEEP WATER: wet, rainy conditions on the road.

DEFINITELY: positive intent or agreement.

DELTA TUNE: a control on some CB rigs which permits tuning the receiving frequence slightly off the center to compensate for variations in transmitting frequency of other transceivers.

DERBY CITY (or TOWN): Louisville, Kentucky (MW).

DESERT STATE: Arizona

DETROIT VIBRATORS: Chevrolets.

DIAMOND IN THE ROUGH: police car stopped on the side of the road (SW).

DIARRHEA OF THE MOUTH: talkative (W).

DICE CITY: Las Vegas, Nevada (W).

DIESEL CAR: tractor trailer truck.

DIESEL DIGIT: Channel 15.

DIG (or DIG IT)?:   do you understand?

DIG YOU OUT: understand you (SE).

DIGGIN' MY SPURS: driving to a destination as fast as possible.

DIME CHANNEL: Channel 10.

DING-A-LING: CBer who speaks without thinking first; person who sounds dumb.

DIP STICK: term for CBer, implying either animosity or affection.

DIRT FLOOR: unpaved parking lot.

DIRTY CITY: Cleveland, Ohio.

DIRTY SIDE (THE):   New York City; New Jersey; the East Coast.

DIRTY WITH BEARS: area filled with police.

DIVORCE CITY: Las Vegas, Nevada (W).

DIXIE CUP: CB operator (female) who speaks with a Southern drawl.

DIXIE TOWN: New Orleans, Louisiana.

DO IT TO IT: drive full speed.

DO IT TO IT LIKE SONNY PRUITT: sign-off.

DO IT TO ME: answer back (SE).

DO YOU COPY?:   do you understand?

DO YOU HAVE A COPY?:   do you hear and understand me?

DO YOU HEAR SOMEONE KNOCKING ON YOUR BACK DOOR?:   I'm about to pass you.

DO YOU READ ME?: do you understand?

DOCK-WALLOPER: dockworker who unloads freight from vehicles.

DOCTOR TOWN: Rochester, Minnesota.

DOG: truck without much power.

DOG HOUSE: cover over big engine (NW).

DOIN' IT TO IT: full speed (SE); e.g. "We doin' it to it and comin' your way."

DOIN' IT TO IT, THAT WAY: sign-off (SE).

DOING OUR THING IN THE LEFTHAND LANE: full speed in the passing lane; sign-off (SE).

DOING THE FIVE-FIVE: driving at 55 miles per hour; e.g. "The bears are crawling on this ol' super slab today; I been doing the five-five for an hour."

DOME CITY: Houston, Texas.

DON'T FEED THE BEARS: don't get a speeding ticket.

DON'T LET YOUR TRICKING TRIP UP YOUR TRUCKING: sign-off (SE).

DON'T LET YOUR TRUCKING TRIP UP YOUR TRICKING: sign-off (SE).

DONUTS: truck tires.

DOUBLE BARREL: radar covering both sides of the road.

DOUBLE BUFFALO: 55 miles per hour.

DOUBLE 18: two 18-wheelers driving side by side.

DOUBLE EIGHTY-EIGHTS: love and kisses.

DOUBLE FIVER: 55 mph.

DOUBLE "L": telephone.

DOUBLE NICKEL: 55 miles per hour.

DOUBLE NICKEL HIGHWAY: Interstate 55 (SE).

DOUBLE SEVEN: no; negative contact; e.g. "Double seven on that Country Bunny."

DOUBLE-TROUBLE: double tractor trailer rig, with two 'boxes' (NE).

DOUBLE-UP: jackknife.

DOWN: sign-off; through transmitting.

DOWN AND GONE: sign-off; turning off the CB (SE, MW).

DOWN AND ON THE SIDE: through talking but monitoring.

DOWN AND OUT OF IT: sign-off.

DOWN FOR THE COUNT: sleeping (NE).

DOWN, OUT, AND ON THE SIDE: sign-off; through transmitting but monitoring.

DOZING: stopped; parked.

DRAG DOWN: shift to lower gears too slowly.

DRAG YOUR FEET: wait a few seconds before transmitting to see if anyone else wants to break into conversation.

DRAGGIN' IT OUT BEHIND: very tired (SW).

DRAGGIN' WAGON: wrecker; tow truck.

DRAIN THE RADIATOR: restroom stop.

DRAPE APE: child (SW).

DRESS FOR SALE: prostitute (SW).

DRESSED FOR THE BALL: CBer monitoring attentively.

DRIVEWAY: short stretch of road.

DRIVING THE PEG: driving the legal speed limit.

DROP CARRIER: stop transmitting for a short time.

DROP THE HAMMER DOWN: accelerate; no police or obstructions ahead; e.g. "Drop the hammer down and bring it thisaway."

DROPOUT: fading of signal during transmission.

DROPPED A CARRIER: keyed the microphone, preventing transmission.

DROPPED IT OFF THE SHOULDER: ran off the side of the highway (SE).

DUCK PLUCKER: obscene term (euphemism).

DUDLEY DO-RIGHT: Missouri highway police.

DUMMY: unmanned police car; e.g. "Watch for the dummy in the median at milepost 216."

DUMMY CAR: empty police car parked as a decoy.

DUMP CHUMP: driver of a dump truck.

DUMP 'ER IN: begin transmitting, I'm turning it over to you.

DUSTED MY BRITCHES: passed me (SE, SW).

DUSTED YOUR EARS: transmission interrupted (SE).

DUSTING: driving all or partly on the road's shoulder, causing a cloud of dust behind.

EIA: Electronic Industries Association.

E-R-P: effective radiated power. The E-R-P may be greater or less than the power generated by the transmitter, depending on antenna system gain or loss.

E.R.S.:   Emergency Radio Service; Channel 9.

EAR ACHE: antenna problems (S).

EARS: CB radio; dual antennas.

EARS ON: CB radio turned on; e.g. "Got your ears on, good buddy?"

*EAST*BOUND, STRUTTIN' STYLE: headed (east) at a high rate of speed; sign-off.

*EAST*BOUND, TRAILER TRUCKIN' STYLE: headed (east) in a tractor truck; sign-off.

EASTER BUNNY: innocent or naive motorist or other person.

EASY CHAIR: middle CB vehicle in a line of three or more (NW).

EATUM-UP-STOP: roadside restaurant.

EIGHT-MILER: driver who hogs the left lane.

8-0-7:   beer.

EIGHTEEN-LEGGED POGO STICK: 18-wheel tractor trailer truck (MW).

EIGHTEEN-WHEELER: tractor trailer truck.

EIGHTS: sign-off; best wishes.

EIGHTS AND OTHER GOOD NUMBERS: best wishes; sign-off.

EIGHTY-EIGHTS: love and kisses; sign-off.

EIGHTY-EIGHTS AROUND THE HOUSE: good luck and best wishes to you and yours; sign-off.

ELECTRIC TEETH: police radar (SE).

ELEVEN-METER BAND: the 27 MHz citizens band, formerly the eleven-meter amateur band.

EMERGENCY VEHICLE: ambulance.

ENVELOPE: unmarked police car (used with color) e.g. "There's a smokey in a blue envelope."

ERECTOR SET: bridge (NE).

EVEL KNIEVEL: motorcyclist.

EVEL KNIEVEL SMOKEY: motorcycle police (SW).

EVERYBODY MUST BE WALKING THE DOG: all channels are busy (SE).

EVERYTHING IS SLICK: the way is clear.

EXPRESSWAY BOOGIE: making a long haul trip.

EXTRA MONEY TICKET: speeding ticket (W).

EYE IN THE SKY: police helicopter.

EYEBALL: meet a CBer in person; have a person in sight.

EYEBALL IT: meet; look (SE); e.g. "When that thunder chicken comes 'round ya, eyeball it one time."

EYEBALL TO EYEBALL: meeting of two CBers together (SE, SW).

EYEBALLS: headlights.

FCC: Federal Communications Commission.

FAKE BRAKE: driver who brakes on and off repeatedly.

FAME TOWN: Canton, Ohio.

FANCY SEAT COVER: pretty girl in passing car.

FARGO LAND: Fargo, North Dakota.

FAT DADDY: truck carrying overload of freight.

FAT LOAD: overload, more weight than local state law allows.

FEATHER FOOT: driver moving too slowly (SE).

FED: inspector (D.O.T. or FCC).

FEED THE BEARS: get caught speeding; e.g. "Don't feed the bears this trip."

FEED THE PONIES (or HORSES): lose money at the horse races (SW).

FEET: linear amplifier; tires.

FENDER BENDER: traffic accident; wreck.

FER SURE: definitely.

FETCH 'EM UP: police chase car (NE).

FIFTY DOLLAR LANE: passing lane (SE).

FINAL: last transmission; e.g. "We'll be clear there with you, on your final."

FINGER-LICKING GOOD: good-looking person.

FINGER WAVE: obscene gesture (SE).

FINGERS: CBer who changes from channel to channel.

FIREWORKS: police vehicle with flashing lights.

FIRST SERGEANT: wife (W).

FISH: Plymouth Barracuda (SE); company executive.

FISHING POLE AND A PARTNER: dual antennas.

FIVE-AND-NINE: strong radio signal coming over clearly.

FIVE-BY-FIVE: good clear signal.

FIVE-BY-NINE: strong radio signal coming over clearly.

FIVE-FINGER DISCOUNT: stolen goods.

FIVE-FIVE: 55 miles per hour; loud, clear signal.

FIVE-TWO: half-baked 10-4.

FIVE WATTS: legal power output for CB set.

FIVES-A-PAIR: 55 mph speed limit.

FIX: police location report.

FIX OR REPAIR DAILIES: Ford trucks.

FIXED STATION: radio station at a fixed location.

FLAG CITY (or TOWN):   road under construction.

FLAG TOWN: Philadelphia, Pennsylvania (NE).

FLAG WAVER: road construction worker.

FLAG-WAVER TAXI: highway repair truck.

FLAKE: person (positive or negative connotation, depending on inflection and person discussed) (MW); one who misuses CB (MW).

FLAKEY: person acting rude, nuts, or mean (NE); euphemism for four-letter words.

FLAPPERS: ears (NW).

FLAPS DOWN: slow down.

FLAT BACK: tractor trailer with unenclosed trailer.

FLAT SIDE: sleep.

FLATBED: tractor trailer truck with unenclosed trailer.

FLEAS ON 'YA: best wishes (slang for three's on you) (NE).

FLICK: movie.

FLIGHT MAN: weigh station worker on wheels (SE, SW, W).

FLIP or FLIP-FLOP: make a U-turn; change direction; return trip; e.g. "Enjoyed the modulation, good buddy, catch you on the flip"; other side of the road.

FLIP-FLOPPING BEARS: police reversing direction; e.g. "Watch them flip-flopping bears at Exit 143 cuz' they be going every whichaway."

FLIPPER: return trip; change direction.

FLOATER: truck driver who doesn't have a steady job.

FLOATS: large single tires on a truck instead of dual tires.

FLOP BOX: motel or hotel room.

FLOP IT: turn around (SE).

FLUFF STUFF: snow.

FLY IN THE SKY: police helicopter; law enforcement aircraft.

FLY PAPER: newly-oiled blacktop on the road; soft blacktop due to hot weather.

FLYING ORDERS: instructions issued to truck driver by dispatcher.

FOG LIFTER: interesting CBer.

FOLDING CAMERA: the in-car speed monitor in some trooper cars.

FOOT IN THE CARBURETOR: police following; travelling at high speed.

FOOT WARMER: linear amplifier.

FOR SURE: definitely.

FORTY-D?:   do you understand?

FORTY-FOOTER: tractor trailer truck (18-wheeler).

FORTY-FOURS: children (SW); kisses.

FORTY-OVER: very strong signal.

FORTY ROGER: O.K.; message received.

FORTY WEIGHT: beer (SW).

FOUR: abbreviation of 10-4 meaning yes; O.K., I understand; do you understand?

FOUR-BY-FOUR: Jeep, Bronco, or Blazer having a 4' x 4' cargo area.

FOUR D: yes; O.K. message received; a variation of 10-4.

FOUR LANE PARKING LOT: crowded expressway (W).

FOUR-LEGGED BEAST: race horse (W).

FOUR-LEGGED GO-GO DANCERS: pigs (SE).

FOUR ROGER: message received; yes.

FOUR-TEN: 10-4, emphatically.

FOUR-TEN ROGER: hello, yes; O.K.; I understand; certainly.

FOUR-WHEELED LOG: skateboard (NE).

FOUR-WHEELER: car; small 4-wheel truck.

FOUR-WHEELER WITH FIRE IN HIS TAIL: speeding car without CB.

FOX CHARLEY: FCC.

FOX HUNTING: FCC looking for CBers who use profane language or otherwise break FCC regulations; e.g. "Uncle Charley's gone fox hunting in Hot Lanta tonight."

FOXY JAWS: CB operator with a sexy voice.

FOXY LADY: attractive woman.

FREE RIDE: prostitute (W).

FREIGHT LIGHT: flashing police lights.

FREQ: frequency (MW).

FREQUENCY SYNTHESIZER: a circuit which enables radio operator to transmit and receive on a number of channels without separate crystals for each function and channel.

FRIENDLY CANDY COMPANY: FCC (NE).

FRIENDLY COUSIN CHARLEY: FCC.

FRIENDLY TERRITORY: road clear of police, radar.

FRILLY BLOUSE: attractive woman.

FRISCO: San Francisco, California.

FRONT DOOR: first CB vehicle in a line of two or more watches for police, obstructions; e.g. "We got that one Red Pepper running the front door for us."

FRONT DOOR, BACK DOOR, ROCKING CHAIR: the front door and the back door are the road ahead and behind. The lead vehicle in a convoy watches the "front door," the rear watches the back, and those in the middle are "in the rocking chair."

FRONT END: first CB vehicle in a line of two or more watches for police, obstructions (MW).

FRONT YARD: road ahead; first CB vehicle in a line of two or more watches for police, obstructions.

FRUITLINER: truck made by White.

FUBAR: foul-up (abbreviation for Fouled Up Beyond All Recognition) (SW).

FUGITIVE: CBer using different channel from his usual.

FULL OF VITAMINS: big engine (SE).

FUN CITY: New Orleans, Louisiana; New York City (NE).

FUNNY BOOKS: pornography.

FUNNY BUNNY: police car in disguise.

FUNNY CANDY COMPANY: FCC.

FUZZ BUSTER: device for detecting radar.

G-B-Y: God Bless You.

GRS: Canadian General Radio Service.

GALOSHES: linear amplifier.

GAMBLING TOWN: Las Vegas, Nevada.

GANDY DANCER: road construction worker.

GAPER'S   BLOCK: traffic   jam   caused   by rubberneckers stopping to look at accident or break-down.

GAPIN' SKIRT: unlocked or open rear door.

GARBAGE: interference on the channel; litter (MW).

GARBAGE MOUTH: one who uses obscene or profane language (NE).

GARBAGEMAN: litterbug (MW).

GATEWAY CITY; THE GATEWAY: St. Louis, Missouri (MW).

GATEWAY TO THE WEST: St. Louis, Missouri.

'GATING: tailgating; vehicle following too closely.

GEAR BONGER: driver who grinds the gears when shifting up or down.

GEAR JAMMER: trucker; driver who grinds the gears frequently.

GEORGE WALLACE COUNTRY: Alabama (SE).

GEORGIA OVERDRIVE: neutral gear.

GESTAPO: federal agents.

GET HORIZONTAL: sleep; go to bed (W).

GET TRUCKING: make some distance (SE).

GETTING OFF (or ON) THE GREEN STAMP: leaving (or entering) a toll road.

GETTING OUT: being heard; clear reception.

GHENGIS KHAN: bad mechanic.

GHOST TALKING: can only hear one person of conversation (S).

GHOST TOWN: Caspar, Wyoming.

GIGGLE JUICE: gas (SW).

GIMME FIVE: speak with me for a few minutes on the CB; shake hands.

GINNING AND GOT THE WHEELS SPINNING: full speed (SE).

GIRLIE BEAR: policewoman (SE).

GIVE ME A SHOT: answer back; call on the CB (SE); e.g. "When you go through that Exit 172, give me a shot. 10-4?"

GIVE ME A SHOUT (or SHOUT, SHOUT): answer back; call on the CB (SE).

GLORY CARD: CB license (NE).

GLORY ROLL: names of CBers known nationally (NW).

GO AHEAD: permission to speak on channel; e.g. "You got the Tennessee Beaver Pleaser, go ahead."

GO BACK TO HIM: talk to him again; answer back.

GO BREAK 10 *(or other channel #)*: permission to speak on channel.

GO BREAKER: permission to speak on channel.

GO-GO GIRLS: load of pigs headed for market.

GO JUICE (or GO-GO JUICE): gas; fuel.

GO 'ROUND: another turn at transmitting.

GO 10-100: restroom stop (W).

GOAT 'N SHOAT MAN: trucker hauling live animals.

GOING DOWN: sign-off; turning off the CB.

GOING-HOME HOLE: high gear.

GOING THATAWAY: going away from home; sign-off.

GOING THISAWAY: going towards home.

GOING WITH THE GRAIN: travelling on pep pills (SW).

GOLDEN ARCHWAYS: St. Louis, Missouri.

GONE: through transmitting (SE); e.g. "The one Sugar Britches, KXI-7248, we be gone;" sign-off.

GONE 10-7 PERMANENTLY: deceased.

GOOD BUDDY: fellow CBer; term or greeting originally used by truckers but now used by most highway CBers; friend.

GOOD NUMBERS: best wishes; e.g. "We'll be putting the good numbers on you and yours."

GOOD PAIR: best wishes (pair of eights).

GOOD SHOT: road clear of police and obstructions.

GOOD TRUCKIN':   drive safely.

GOODIED UP: truck made to look fancy.

GOODIES: accessories for the CB (NW).

GOON SQUAD: group of CBers hogging the channel (NE).

GOT A COPY?:   do you hear?; e.g. "Anybody got a copy on this One-Eyed Tom?"

GOT A 10-2:   obtaining a clear reception.

GOT HIS SHOES ON: full speed (SE).

GOT MY EYEBALLS PEELED: I'm looking (SE).

GOT MY FOOT ON IT: accelerating (SE).

GOT THE COPY?:   did you understand?

GOT YOUR EARS ON?:   are you listening?

GOURD HEAD: take the channel; go ahead and transmit (MW).

GRAB BAG: make a general call to anyone on channel (NE).

GRAB BAGGING: police at a speed trap issuing tickets.

GRAB ONE: shift into lower gear when driving uphill to get extra power.

GRANDMA: lowest gear, or combination of gears, that driver uses to get extra power.

GRANDSTAND JOCKEY: driver who is careless or shows off.

GRANNY GEAR: lowest gear.

GRAPEFRUIT: overly cautious vehicle.

GRASS: median; e.g. "How about you Eastbound, you got a bear in the grass at Exit 202, 10-4?"; marijuana.

GRASSHOPPER: park policeman.

GREASY: slick or icy road (NE).

GREAT BIG SPROCKET: big engine (SE).

GREEN APPLE: new, inexperienced CBer.

GREEN CBer: military police with CB (W).

GREEN LIGHT: road clear of police and obstructions; e.g. "10-4 guy, you be havin' a green light all the way to that Circle City."

GREEN LIGHT AND A WHITE LINE: road clear of police and obstructions; drive desired speed.

GREEN LOLLIPOP: milepost (SW).

GREEN MACHINE: marine base.

GREEN STAMP: toll road (NE); toll booth (NE).

GREEN STAMP COLLECTOR: police with radar giving out tickets.

GREEN STAMP LANE: passing lane (SE).

GREEN STAMP ROAD: toll road.

GREEN STAMPS: speeding tickets; money.

GREENS: speeding tickets; money (SE).

GROUND CLOUDS: fog.

GROWED-UP TRUCK: tractor trailer rig (SE).

GUARANTOLD YOU: guaranteed; I told you the truth.

GUITAR CITY: Kalamazoo, Michigan.

GUITAR TOWN: Nashville, Tennessee (SE, MW).

GUMBALL MACHINE: emergency vehicle with flashing lights on top.

GUN RUNNER: police radar (SE).

GUNNY BAG: quit working (NW).

GUNNYBEGGER: friendly term CBers use for each other (MW).

GUTTER BALLING: bowling (W).

GUY: fellow trucker (MW, NE); unidentified CBer.

GYPSY: independent trucker; trucker who owns his own rig; trucker who trip-leases to authorized carriers.

H & D: hate and dissent.

H TOWN: Hopkinsville, Kentucky (MW, SE).

HACK: taxicab.

HAG BAG: female bum.

HAG FEAST: female CBers hogging channel (NE).

HAGFEST: group of female CBers conversing on the channel.

HAIRCUT PALACE: bridge or overpass with low clearance (MW).

HALLOWEEN MACHINE: Cooper-Jarrett truck.

HAM: amateur radio operator.

HAMBOREE: jamboree for radio hams.

HAMBURGER HELPER: linear amplifier (W).

HAMFEST: get-together or jamboree for ham operators.

HAMMER: accelerator.

HAMMER BACK: slow down.

HAMMER DOWN: accelerating; highballing.

HAMMER HANGING: accelerating; same as hammer down.

HAMMER JAMMER: car trouble (SE).

HAMMER OFF: slow down (NE).

HAMMER ON: accelerate (NE).

HAMMER UP: slow down; police or obstruction ahead.

HAMMING: using the CB channels for gossip, talking about hobbies.

HANDIE-TALKIE: portable CB set with its own antenna and battery pack.

HANDLE: code name CBer uses in transmission; e.g. "The Stripper," "Jungle Jim," "Licketty Split," "Peanuts," "Bon Bon," "Dew Drop."

HANDSET: microphone and earphone in one unit, used like a telephone.

HANG A RIGHT (or LEFT): turn right (or left) (MW).

HANG IT IN YOUR EAR: nonsense (W).

HANG MY NEEDLE: receiving strong signal and clear reception.

HANG OUT: monitor a specific channel.

HANGAR: garage.

HAPPY NUMBERS: best wishes to you.

HARD ANKLE: working man; trucker.

HARD TO PULL OUT: hard to understand.

HARVEY WALLBANGER: reckless driver (MW).

HASH: interference on the channel.

HASH AND TRASH: background noise; signal unclear (W).

HAULING POST HOLES: driving a truck or trailer without freight.

HAVE A SAFE ONE AND A SOUND ONE: drive safely (SE).

HAVE A 36-24-36 TONIGHT: sign-off.

HAVE YOURSELF A GOOD DAY TODAY AND A BETTER DAY TOMORROW: sign-off.

HAVE YOURSELF A SAFE ONE AND A FINE ONE: drive safely.

HAVEN'T SEEN A THING IN YOUR LANE: the way is clear on your side.

HEATER: linear amplifier which boosts CB output.

HEAVY FOOT: driving below the posted speed.

HEMORRHOID WITH A POLAROID: police on your bumper with radar (MW, SE).

HENCHMEN: group of CBers (NW).

HE'S LAYIN', HE'S STAYIN':   making the best time possible with the equipment he has; through transmitting but monitoring.

HIDING IN THE BUSHES, SITTING UNDER THE LEAVES: hidden police car (SE).

HIDING IN THE GRASS: police car on median (SE).

HIGH GEAR: use of linear amplifier, an illegal piece of equipment which increases output to several hundred watts.

HIGH RISE: bridge or overpass with high clearance.

HIGH WATER: Great Falls, Montana.

HIGHBALLING: driving fast; accelerating.

HILL TOWN: San Francisco, California.

HILLBILLY OPERA HOUSE: CB radio.

HILLBILLY WAGON: White Freightliner.

HIND END: last CB vehicle in a line of two or more (SE, SW).

HIP POCKET: glove compartment.

HIT ME ONE TIME: answer back so I'll know my radio is transmitting.

HIT THE HAY: go to bed.

HIT THE RACK: go to bed.

HIT THE SHEETS: go to bed (SE).

HIT THE SNORE SHELF: go to bed.

HOG COUNTRY: Arkansas (SE).

HOLDING ON TO YOUR MUD FLAPS: driving close behind you (MW).

HOLE IN THE WALL: tunnel; Baltimore, Maryland.

HOLE IN THE WALL RATS: Tunnel Authority Police (New York City).

HOLLER: a call for a specific person on the CB set; e.g. "Give me a holler next time you're on the ol' channel."

HOLY CITY: Palestine, Texas (SW).

HOME CHANNEL: channel which two or more CBers select for their conversation.

HOME ON ITS BACK: camper.

HOME PORT: residence location (SE).

HOME TWENTY: residence location; e.g. "What's your home twenty on that end?"

HONEY: beer (SE).

HONEY BEAR: female state trooper.

HONEY WAGON: beer truck (SE).

HONEYMOON: driver's first trip in a new truck.

HOO HOONER: driver who hogs the left-hand lane.

HOOD LIFTER: garage mechanic.

HOOSIER STATE: Indiana.

HORIZONTAL: asleep.

HORIZONTALLY POLARIZED: asleep in bed; electric field of antenna parallel to the earth's horizon.

HORSE: Ford Mustang or Colt (SE, SW); tractor trailer truck (MW).

HOT FOOT: added power on a CB set (NW).

HOT LANTA: Atlanta, Georgia (SE).

HOT LOAD: shipment of freight to be hauled in a rush.

HOT 'N HEAVY: strong signal.

HOT PANTS: smoke; fire.

HOT STUFF: coffee (SE).

HOT TOWN: Atlanta, Georgia (SE).

HOT WATER CITY: Hot Springs, Arkansas.

HOUND DOG: radar chase car (NE).

HOUND ON THE GROUND: police car (NE).

HOUSE: truck trailer.

HOW ABOUT AN *EAST*BOUND (or *NORTH, SOUTH, WEST*BOUND):   call for a CBer going direction indicated.

HOW ABOUT IT?:   okay?

HOW ABOUT THAT (*handle*) ONE TIME?:   call for a specific CBer (SE); e.g. "How about that Tumbleweed one time?"

HOW ABOUT YOU (*handle*)?:   call for a specific CBer.

HOW ABOUT YOUR VOCAL CHORDS?:   is your set operating? (SE).

HOW AM I HITTING YOU?: how do you receive my transmission?

HOW DO YOU READ ME?:   what is the meter reading on my transmission?

HOW TALL ARE YOU?: what is the height of your truck? (MW).

HOW WE BE LOOKING BACK YOUR WAY?: is the highway clear the way I'm going?

HOW YOU BE?: how are you?

HOWZIT: how are you? how are things going with you?

HUMP: mountain.

HUNDRED MILE COFFEE: strong coffee.

HUNG UP: must continue to monitor the CB.

HUSTLER: brand name of antenna; also any antenna.

HYDROPLANE: skid on puddles.

I-C-X: ice cream express.

I.D.: identification; proper identification of station using callsign.

ICEBERG (THE): Anchorage, Alaska.

IDIOT BOX: television set.

IF YOU CAN'T USE IT, ABUSE IT: masturbate (MW).

IF YOU GOT THE DESIRE, SET YOUR WHEELS ON FIRE: the way is clear, speed if you want to.

I'M THROUGH: sign-off; through transmitting.

IN A SHORT, SHORT: soon (SE); e.g. "I'll be back on the rip strip in a short, short."

IN THE CLEAR: sign-off for the time being; no interference coming over now.

IN (or UNDER) THE DOGHOUSE: under the hood of a vehicle.

IN THE GRASS: in the median (SE).

IN THE HOLE: pulled over or arrested by the police.

IN THE MUD: transmission not coming clearly, interference equals strength of your transmission.

IN THE PEN: parked; CB set not in use.

INDIANS: neighbors who get interference on television because of CB transmission (comes from Tennessee Valley Indians).

INSTAMATIC: radar set-up.

INVITATION: traffic ticket.

IRISH CITY: South Bend, Indiana.

IRON: old truck.

IRON LUNGER: 220 or 250 horsepower engine.

IRON TOWN: Cleveland, Ohio.

IVY TOWN: Providence, Rhode Island.

J TOWN: Jackson, Tennessee (SE).

J TRAIL: CB jamboree season, usually February to November.

JACK IT UP: accelerate (SE); e.g. "Jack it up and brought yourself on up here."

JACK RABBIT: police of any kind (W).

JACKING IT AROUND: backing up a semi-trailer around a very sharp curve.

JAILBAIT: desirable girl below the legal age of consent.

JAM: deliberately interfere with station to block out transmission.

JAMBOREE: large gathering of CBers, often including camp-outs, entertainment, and door prizes.

JAMMED OUT: station blocked out by interference, probably caused deliberately.

JAPANESE TOY: CB radio.

JAVA: coffee.

JAWJACKING: talking on the CB (MW).

JAWS: animal in vehicle (MW).

JAZZ CITY: New Orleans, Louisiana.

JIMMIE: a type of tractor trailer truck engine; White Freightliner; GMC truck (NE).

JOCK: male.

JOHN LAW: police of any kind.

JOY JUICE: liquor.

JUICE: gasoline or diesel fuel; liquor.

JUICE JUG: gas tank (MW).

JUKE JOINT: inexpensive restaurant or bar.

JUMP DOWN: switch to a lower CB channel.

JUMP UP: switch to a higher CB channel.

JUMPIN' BEAN: karate expert (SE).

JUNKYARD: place of employment.

K TOWN: Knoxville, Tennessee (SE).

K. C. TOWN: Kansas City, Missouri and Kansas.

K-WHOMPER: Kenworth truck (NE).

KANGAROO(ING): bouncing load; loose load; e.g. "You northbound portable floor fourteen-wheeler, you've got a kangaroo loose on the parking side."

KEEP 'EM BETWEEN THE DITCHES: drive safely (SE).

KEEP ON TRUCKING: keep going; sign-off.

KEEP STROKING: good luck and best wishes (NE).

KEEP THE ANTENNA WIGGLIN' AND THE GIRLS GIGGLIN': sign-off.

KEEP THE BEAVERS IN YOUR LAP AND THE BEARS OFF YOUR BACK AND YOU HAVE YOURSELF A FINE DAY: sign-off (NE).

KEEP THE BUGS OFF THE GLASS AND THE BEARS OFF YOUR TAIL: sign-off.

KEEP THE ROLLING SIDE DOWN AND THE SHINY SIDE UP: drive safely (SE); sign-off.

KEEP THE RUBBER SIDE DOWN: drive safely; sign-off.

KEEP THE SHINY SIDE UP AND THE DIRTY SIDE DOWN: drive safely; sign-off (MW).

KEEP THE SHINY SIDE UP AND THE GREASY SIDE DOWN: drive safely (NW); sign-off.

KEEP THE SHINY SIDE UP AND THE ROLLING SIDE DOWN: drive safely; sign-off.

KEEP THE WHEELS SPINNING: drive safely (SE).

KEEP YOUR NOSE BETWEEN THE DITCHES AND SMOKEY OUT OF YOUR BRITCHES: drive safely and look out for speed traps and speeding fines; sign-off.

KEEP YOUR WHEELS OUT OF THE DITCHES AND THE SMOKEYS OUT OF YOUR BRITCHES: drive safely and don't get any speeding tickets; sign-off.

KEEP YOUR WHEELS SPINNING AND THE BEAVERS GRINNING: drive safely and keep the girls happy; sign-off.

KENOSHA CADILLAC: any car made by AMC.

KEY: activate the microphone by pressing button.

KEYBOARD: controls on CB radio.

KEYING THE MIKE: activating the microphone without speaking.

KICK: turn the channel over to someone.

KICK DOWN: downshift to a lower gear.

KICK THE DONUTS: check the tires.

KICKER: linear amplifier.

KIDDIE CAN: school bus (SE).

KIDDIE CAR: school bus (SE); e.g. "What about that Northbound side, you got a kiddie car at milepost 116; better back 'em on down. 10-4?"

KIDNEY BUSTER: truck that is uncomfortable to ride in.

KITTY WHOMPER: Kenworth truck (NE).

KNOCK IT ABOUT: the way is clear; drive desired speed.

KNOCK THE SLACK OUT: accelerate (SE).

KNOCKING: vehicle moving as best it can.

KNUCKLE BUSTER: fight (W).

KODAK: police radar (SE).

KODIAK WITH A KODAK: police with radar.

KOJAK: state trooper (SE); e.g. "There's a Kojak with a kodak at Exit 43, better back 'em on down."

KOJAK WITH A KODAK: state trooper with radar.

KOOL AID: liquor; beer (SE, SW).

L-S-B: lower sideband.

LADY BEAR: policewoman.

LADY BREAKER: female CB operator asking for channel.

LAME: stopped because of broken-down vehicle; e.g. "I'm lame at post 211 on Route 10 northbound."

LAND LINE: telephone.

LAND OF DISNEY: Disneyland, California (W).

LAND OF WONDERFUL: road is clear of police and obstructions (SE).

LATCH-ON: vehicle without CB following one so equipped (SE).

LATRINE LIPS: one who uses profane or obscene language on the CB (W).

LAUGHIN' CITY: Longmont, Colorado.

LAY AN EYE ON IT: see it.

LAY DOWN: stop transmitting so someone else can speak.

LAY IT ON ME: tell me about it.

LAY IT OVER: through talking but monitoring (stand by) (SE).

LAY IT TO THE FLOOR: accelerate; full speed.

LAY ON THE AIR: put on the brakes.

LAY OVER AND LISTEN: through transmitting but monitoring.

LEAD FOOT: driving below the posted speed limit.

LEFT LANE: passing lane.

LEFT SHOULDER: opposite direction; police situation and road condition; e.g. "Thanks for the come back, good buddy, how's it lookin' over your left shoulder?"

LEGAL BEAGLE: one who uses the correct and legal callsign and abides by FCC rules (W).

LEGALIZE: slow down to the speed limit; e.g. "Better get legalized, guy, smokey's ahead at milepost 208."

LEGALIZING *EAST* (*or other direction*): driving east legally (or other direction).

LET IT GO: accelerate to desired speed (MW).

LET IT ROLL: accelerate; e.g. "The way is clean so let it roll, good buddy."

LET THE CHANNEL ROLL: let others break in and use the channel.

LET THE HAMMER DOWN: full speed; road is clear of police and obstructions.

LET THE MOTOR TOTE 'ER: accelerate.

LET THE PEDAL HIT THE METAL: accelerate (SE).

LET YOUR FLAPS DOWN: slow down (SE).

LETTUCE: money (W).

LIBERTY CITY: Philadelphia, Pennsylvania.

LICORICE STICK: blacktop road that has many twists and turns.

LID: inept radio operator; dumb person.

LIE SHEET: trucker's log sheet.

LIGHT FOOTIN' IT: driving the legal speed limit.

LIGHT'S GREEN: road is clear of police and obstructions.

LIGHT'S GREEN, BRING ON THE MACHINE: road is clear of police and obstructions; drive at desired speed.

LIL' OL' MODULATOR: CB set.

LIMA: telephone patch.

LINCOLN COUNTRY: Illinois.

LINEAR: linear amplifier to boost CB output.

LINEAR AMPLIFIER: illegal piece of gear which increases output to several hundred watts.

LINEAR LUNGS: CBer who broadcasts in a loud voice (NW).

LIT CANDLES: police car with flashing lights.

LITTLE BEARS: local police (SE).

LITTLE BIT: prostitute; sexual activity (SE, MW); e.g. "There's always a little bit at that truck 'em up stop about this time."

LITTLE FOOT WARMER: linear amplifier or power booster.

LITTLE HELP: added power.

LITTLE HERE, A LITTLE THERE, YOU GOTTA WATCH OUT FOR SMOKEY THE BEAR: sign-off.

LITTLE MAMA: short antenna.

LITTLE PONIES: small beers.

LITTLE TWIN (THE): Duluth, Minnesota; Superior, Wisconsin.

LITTLE TWINS: Fargo, North Dakota.

LIVIN' DEAD: tailgaters or tailgating.

LOAD: cargo; freight.

LOAD OF POST HOLES: empty truck.

LOAD OF ROCKS: truck hauling bricks (NW).

LOAD OF SAILBOAT WIND: truck running empty.

LOAD OF STICKS: truck hauling cut timber (NW).

LOADED FOR BEAR: vehicle is equipped with a CB radio for listening to police location reports.

LOADED WITH SAILBOAT FUEL: running empty.

LOADED WITH VOLKSWAGEN RADIATORS: running empty.

LOCAL BEARS: local police.

LOCAL BOY: local police (SE).

LOCAL CONSTABULARY: police officers of a small town.

LOCAL SMOKEL: local police (NE).

LOCAL SMOKEY: local police.

LOCAL YOKEL: local police (SE).

LOG: listing of communications a CBer has had, recording pertinent information including handle, callsign, and location.

LOG SOME Z's: get some sleep.

LOGGING CAPITOL: Washington state.

LOLLIPOP: microphone; milepost (SW); homosexual (MW).

LONG ARM: police.

LONG DISTANCE TELEPHONE IS RINGING: call for a specific CBer (SE).

LONGHORN STATE: Texas.

LOOSE BOARDWALK: bumpy road.

LOPING YOUR MULE: masturbating (SW).

LOSER: Mets fan; taxpayer (NE).

LOST WAGES: Las Vegas, Nevada.

LOTION BOTTLE: gas tank.

LOVELAND PASS: top of the Continental Divide (Denver, Colorado).

LUXURY APARTMENT ON WHEELS: mobile home trailer; fancy van (W).

M-O-L: my old lady (SW).

M-O-M: my old man (SW).

MACK CITY: Allentown, Pennsylvania.

MACON TOWN: Macon, Georgia.

MAFIA SQUAD: tough group of truckers.

MAGIC CITY: Birmingham, Alabama.

MAGIC METAL BOX: CB radio.

MAGIC NUMBERS ON YOU: best wishes.

MAGNOLIA STATE: Mississippi (SE).

MAIL: overheard CB conversations; e.g. "I've just been reading the mail tonight."

MAKE A TRIP: switch channels (NW).

MAKE THE TRIP?: is transmission received?

MAKING MOTORS FOR TRICYCLES: making love.

MAKING THE TRIP: sending out a good signal.

MAKING THREE TRACKS IN THE SAND: very tired (SW).

MAMA: wife (SE).

MAMA BEAR: policewoman.

MAMA SMOKEY: female state trooper (SE).

MAMA'S LANE: passing lane; trucker is anxious to get home to mama (wife).

MAN IN A SLICKER: fireman (NW).

MAN IN BLUE: policeman (NW).

MAN IN WHITE: doctor (NW).

MAN WITH A GUN: police with radar (SE).

MANIAC: garage mechanic.

MARDI GRAS TOWN: New Orleans, Louisiana.

MARK-L (or MARKEL) MAN: representative of the Markel Insurance Co. who checks speeding trucks; cannot ticket but can report to company.

MARKER: milepost along expressway, indicating exact location; e.g. "What's your marker now, good buddy?"

MASHING THE MIKE: keying of the microphone without speaking to prevent messages (SE).

MAY ALL YOUR UPS AND DOWNS BE BETWEEN THE SHEETS: sign-off.

McLEAN LANE: right hand lane of expressway; the slow lane.

MEAT WAGON: ambulance (W).

MEETING TWENTY: meeting place.

MELTING THE VOICE COIL: very strong signal coming into the receiver.

MERCY: common expression acknowledging reception of remark; universal euphemism for all the words that are illegal on the air; wow; gee whiz.

MERCY SAKES: common expression acknowledging reception of remark; universal euphemism for all the words that are illegal on the air; wow; gee whiz.

MERCY SNAKES: emphatic statement (euphemism) (MW); e.g. "Mercy snakes alive, look at all the smokies on the I-55."

MEXICAN OVERDRIVE: taking car or truck out of gear to go down grade.

MICKEY MITCHELL: local police (SE).

MICKEY MOUSE METRO ON A TRICYCLE: local police on a three-wheel motorcycle (SE).

MICKEY MOUSE TOWN: Disney World, Florida (SE).

MICRO BUS: van (MW).

MIDNIGHT OVERDRIVE: taking car or truck out of gear to go down grade.

MIDNIGHT SHOPPER: thief.

MIK-E-NIK: mechanic, grease monkey (SW).

MIKE: microphone.

MIKE FRIGHT: condition of being nervous about speaking on the CB.

MILE HIGH CITY (or TOWN):   Denver, Colorado.

MILEMARKER: milepost along expressway, indicating exact location; e.g. "I'm Eastbound on this I-10 at milemarker 186. What's your twenty?"

MILFORD LAND: passing lane.

MILK RUN: easy trip.

MINI SKIRT: woman, girl (SE).

MINI STATE: Rhode Island (NE).

MINNIE: cargo under 100 pounds.

MIRACLE CITY: Conroe, Texas (SW).

MISTAKE ON THE LAKE (THE):   Cleveland, Ohio.

MIX-MASTER: highway cloverleaf (MW); unusually confusing intersection (SW).

MIXING BOWL: highway cloverleaf.

MOBILE: vehicle; CB radio.

MOBILE EYEBALL: look at another truck while driving.

MOBILE MATTRESS: car pulling a camper.

MOBILE PARKING LOT: auto carrier (W).

MOBILE RIG: CB installed in vehicle (car, truck, boat, camper, motorcycle).

MOBILE UNIT: transceiver installed in a vehicle or carried by a person.

MOBILING: going for a ride (W).

MOCCASINS: linear amplifier to boost CB output.

MODJITATE: talk on the CB.

MODULATING: talking; e.g. "Definitely did enjoy modulating with you this mornin' on this ol' base."

MODULATION: talk; voice; conversation.

MODULATION BOOSTER: device or built-in circuit in a CB transceiver which adds gain to a microphone circuit to make it more sensitive, but which automatically limits output to prevent overmodulation.

MOLLIES: pep pills.

MONFORT LANE: passing lane (SW).

MONITOR: listen to the CB; listen to emergency assistance, Channel 9.

MONKEY LOOKING FOR BANANAS AT (*location*): police on the lookout for speeders at location indicated (NE).

MONKEY TOWN: Montgomery, Alabama (SE).

MONSTER: television.

MONSTER LANE: passing lane (MW).

MONTY: Montana.

MOTHBALL: annual CB convention.

MOTION-LOTION: gas; fuel (SE); e.g. "I'm peeling off for some of that motion-lotion; see you on the boulevard in a short, short."

MOTION-POTION: gasoline; fuel.

MOTIVATE: move.

MOTOR CITY: Detroit, Michigan.

MOTORBOATING: fluctuating signal.

MOTORING ON: traveling on (SE).

MOTORMOUTH: one who stays on the CB all the time; one who talks too much.

MOUNTIES IN THE SKY: police helicopter (SE).

MOUNTY: Sheriff's Department.

MOUSE EARS: police car; policeman (SW).

MOVABLE PARKING DECK: auto carrier.

MOVE: vehicle in motion.

MOVIE CAMERA: radar in moving police vehicle.

MOVIES: radar in moving police vehicle.

MOVIN' MOTEL: mobile home trailer; fancy van (W).

MR. CLEAN: over-cautious driver.

M20: meeting place (SE).

MUCK TRUCK: cement truck.

MUCKY-MUCK (or MUCKETY-MUCK): trucking company executive; important person.

MUD: coffee; noise on the channel other than interference.

MUFF: woman; girl.

MUFFIN: attractive girl.

MUSHY: transmission unclear.

MUSIC CITY: Nashville, Tennessee (SE).

MUSICAL CITY: Nashville, Tennessee (SE).

MUSKRATS: children (SE, SW).

MUSQUEETER: insulting term (euphemism).

NCCRA: North Carolina Citizens Radio Association.

NAKED CITY: New York City.

NAP TRAP: motel; rest area.

NASTYVILLE: Nashville, Tennessee (SE).

NATIVES: local CBers in a community.

NATURE BREAK: restroom stop (SE).

NATURE CALL: restroom stop (MW).

NAZI GO-CART: Volkswagen (SE).

NEEDLE CITY: Seattle, Washington.

NEGATINE: no (SE, SW, W).

NEGATIVE: no.

NEGATIVE CONTACT: station called does not respond.

NEGATIVE COPY: no answer; can't understand what you said.

NEGATIVE GROUND: the negative battery terminal of a vehicle is connected to the body and frame.

NEGATORE: no.

NEGATORY: no.

NERVE CURVE: treacherous part of the road; hairpin curves on mountain roads.

NICKEL CHANNEL: Channel 5.

NICKEL'S WORTH: five minute time limit for talking set by the FCC (MW).

NIGHTCRAWLERS: police everywhere (SE).

NINE-TO-FIVERS: regular day workers.

NINER: emergency.

95 IS THE ROUTE YOU'RE ON, IT'S NOT THE SPEED LIMIT SIGN: slow down (used on I-95 from Maine to Florida) (NE, SE).

NINETY WEIGHT: liquor (SW).

NOBODY KNOWS WHERE THE TEDDY BEAR GOES: state troopers are crisscrossing the expressway (SE).

NOD OUT: sleep.

NOISE BLANKER: (see NOISE LIMITER); similar, but chops holes in the signal path ahead of the detector.

NOISE LIMITER: circuit which reduces impulse type noise in a CB receiver by chopping holes in the audio signal path.

NOISE MACHINE: New York City Police Muffler Control (NE).

NOSE DIVE: tractor trailer tips forward on its nose.

NOTHING BUT A GREEN LIGHT AND A WHITE LINE: the way is clear; sign-off.

O.K.: sign-off.

O-M: old man; husband.

O-W: old woman; wife.

OASIS: truck stop.

OCEAN MOUTH: constant talker (NE).

OFF STOP WATCH: behind time (MW).

OIL BURNER: vehicle that is smoking.

OIL CITY: Oklahoma City, Oklahoma.

OKIE: Oklahoma City, Oklahoma.

OLD KITTY WHOMPER: truck (MW).

OLD LADY: wife.

OLD MAN: husband.

OLD (*town name*) TOWN: used for towns and cities without a CB nickname; e.g. "Old Mill River Town."

OMNIDIRECTIONAL ANTENNA: an antenna that radiates equally well in all directions.

ON A (*city name*) TURN: return trip from named city (SE); e.g. "I'm on a Memphis turn." (I will make my return from Memphis.)

ON SKIP: distant signal.

ON STANDBY: monitoring but not transmitting.

ON THE BY: monitoring but not transmitting.

ON THE FLY: moving fast.

ON THE MOVE: vehicle is traveling.

ON THE PAY: at the legal speed limit.

ON THE PEG: at the legal speed limit.

ON THE SIDE: standing by and monitoring; parked or pulled over on the shoulder.

ON THE SIXTY: driving 60 mph.

ON THE STOP WATCH: on time (MW).

ONE IN THE SHOWER, ONE IN THE BATHTUB WATCHING: police car with radar and a chase car up the road (NE).

ONE FOOT ON THE FLOOR, ONE HANGING OUT THE DOOR, AND SHE JUST WON'T DO NO MORE: full speed (SE).

ONE TIME: short contact; right now; e.g. "Give me a 10-13, one time."

ONE-EYED MONSTER: television set.

ONE WAY CAMPER: ambulance; hearse (NE).

OPEN SEASON: police are everywhere (SE).

OPRYLAND: Nashville, Tennessee.

OTHER HALF: wife (usually), or husband; driving partner.

OTHER RADIO: additional radio to scan police channels (NW).

OUR NICKEL IS UP: CB conversation has reached the five minute time limit set by the FCC.

OUT: through transmitting; sign-off.

OUTDOOR TV: drive-in movie (W).

OUTPUT: signal sent out by the CB.

OVER: through transmitting but listening.

OVER THE SHOULDER: the road behind; e.g. "Take a peek over your shoulder, good buddy, and tell me about them ol' smokeys."

OVERMODULATION: talking too long; talking too close to the microphone.

OVERSIZED GRASSHOPPER: lawnmower (MW).

OVERSIZED 'SKEETER: airplane (with or without radar).

P.A. TOWN: Port Arthur, Texas (SW).

P & D's: pickups and deliveries of cargo.

P-C: printed curcuit.

P-E-P: peak envelope power; the power generated by an S-S-B transmitter when modulated.

P-F FLYERS: truck wheels (SE).

P-T-T SWITCH: push-to-talk switch on CB.

PACER: vehicle going first to flush out police (MW).

PACK IT UP: finish for the day.

PACKAGE 'ER UP: signal turned over for you to sign off.

PADIDDLE: vehicle with one headlight.

PAIR OF FIVES: 55 miles per hour; the legal speed limit.

PAIR OF NICKELS: 55 miles per hour.

PAIR OF SEVENS: no contact or answer; e.g. "Pair of sevens on that Roving Rebel."

PAJAMA WAGON: tractor cab with sleeping area.

PANCAKE CITY: Liberal, Kansas.

PANHANDLERS: nurses (MW).

PANIC IN THE STREETS: FCC enforcement apparatus is working the area.

PANTY STRETCHER: fat person.

PAPA BEAR: state trooper with CB (MW).

PAPER: traffic ticket.

PAPER HANGER: police giving speeding tickets (SE, SW, W); CB operator who passes out QSL cards indiscriminately.

PAPERBAG CASE: unattractive female (NE).

PAPERWORK: speeding ticket (SE); e.g. "Smokey's got a four-wheeler on the side at mile marker 113 and he's doing his paperwork."

PARKING LOT: traffic tie-up.

PART 15: FCC Rules applicable to the operation of unlicensed radio transmitter.

PART 95: FCC Rules covering CB service.

PARTY HAT: lights on police car.

PARTY HAT ON: police car with lights flashing.

PARTY HAT ON THE SHELF: lights flashing inside police car (SE).

PASS THE NUMBERS TO YOU: best wishes.

PATCH: city; town (used with name); e.g. "I'm headed for that Newton patch."

PATHFINDER: snow plow.

PAUSE FOR A CAUSE: restroom stop.

PAVEMENT PRINCESS: roadside or truckstop prostitute. They have colorful handles like "Bra Buster" and "Panty Stretcher."

PAY HOLE: high gear.

PEA PICKER: obscene term (euphemism) (NE).

PEACH STATE: Georgia.

PEAK: maximum power.

PEAK POWER: maximum wattage.

PEAKED UP: CB radio putting out more than four watts.

PEANUT BUTTER IN HIS EARS: is not listening (SW).

PEANUT BUTTER THREE: weak transmission surrounded by signals which are stronger.

PEANUT WAGON: large trailer pulled by a small tractor.

PEANUT WHISTLE: CB set with little power; CB without a linear amplifier.

PEDAL: coast; move.

PEDAL A LITTLE SLOWER: slow down (SE).

PEDAL AGAINST THE METAL: driving fast (SE)

PEDAL ALONG AND WAIT ON YOU: coast (SE).

PEDAL DOWN: drive fast; accelerate.

PEDAL PUSHER: bicycle rider (NE).

PEDAL TO THE METAL: gas pedal down to the floor; driving fast.

PEDALING DEAD AND BLIND: driving slowly because driver can't see properly.

PEDALING IN THE MIDDLE: straddling both lanes; riding in the middle lane of a three-lane highway (SE).

PEDALING WITH BOTH FEET: driving a vehicle at top speed.

PEDDLE RUN: truck route having many stops for delivering shipment.

PEEL OFF: make the turn (SE).

PEELING OFF: getting off the expressway (SE); e.g. "We'll be peeling off the expressway at Exit 202."

PEG LEG: driver who brakes and accelerates in a disturbing manner, interrupting movement of traffic.

PEPPER SHAKER: gravel and tar truck used for road repair (NE).

PEPSI DAY: wonderful day; sign-off.

PERSUADER: linear amplifier to boost CB output.

PETE: Peterbilt truck.

PETER RABBIT: police of any kind (W).

PETRO: gasoline.

PETRO REFINERY: truck hauling gas or oil (SW).

PHILLY (or PHILLY TOWN): Philadelphia, Pennsylvania.

PHOTOGRAPHER: police with radar.

PICK 'EM UP TRUCK: pick-up truck.

PICKDOWN: pick-up truck (MW).

PICKLE SUIT: marine uniform (W).

PICKUM-UP: light truck; pick-up truck.

PICNIC: drinking party (alcoholic beverages) (MW).

PICTURE BOX: radar unit.

PICTURE TAKER: police with radar.

PICTURE-TAKING MACHINE: police radar.

PICTURES: radar.

PIECE OF PAPER: speeding ticket.

PIG: policeman, particularly one who oversteps his authority.

PIGEON: motorist caught speeding (SE); e.g. "The smokey at milepost 116 has a pigeon."

PIGEON PLUCKER: police pulling in speeders and issuing tickets.

PIGGY BACK: trailer attached to a car; trailer or container carried by rail.

PIGGY BANK: toll booth (NE, MW).

PIKE: turnpike.

PINE TREE STATE: Maine (NE).

PINK PANTHER: unmarked police car; one with CB (SE).

PINK QSL CARD: warning ticket (SW).

PINK SLIP: warning ticket (SW, W).

PINK TICKET: notice of violation of FCC rules.

PINNIN' THE NEEDLE: coming in with excellent reception.

PIPELINE: specific channel; e.g. "We'll give you a holler on the pipeline tomorrow."

PIT STOP: stop for restroom, food, or fuel.

PITCH A PARAKEET: shoot the bird (an obscene finger gesture) (SE).

PLAIN BROWN (*or other color*) WRAPPER: un-marked police car of color indicated.

PLAY DEAD: stand by on the CB.

PLAY IN THE SANDBOX: use the restroom.

PLUCKING CHICKENS: police at a speed trap pulling in and ticketing motorists.

POKEY: jail.

POLACK 50¢ PIECE: cheap prostitute (NE).

POLACK KIDS: cattle (SE).

POLACK PETERBILT: International Harvester truck (MW).

POLACK SCHOOL BUS: cattle truck (SE).

POLAR BEAR: state trooper.

POLAROID: police radar.

POLE CAT: highway patrol car in black and white (SW).

POLISH HAIRTONIC: tanker truck carrying oil (NE).

POLITZ-EYE: police.

POOP: information.

POPCORN: hail.

PORCUPINE: vehicle with several antennas; vehicle causing annoyance to other drivers.

PORKY BEAR: police of any kind (SE).

PORTABLE BARN YARD: cattle truck.

PORTABLE CAN: long haul tractor trailer carrying liquid; tanker.

PORTABLE CHICKEN COOP: movable weighing scales; movable truck weighing station.

PORTABLE COW: milk truck (SW).

PORTABLE FLOOR: flatbed tractor trailer (SE).

PORTABLE GAS STATION: truck transporting gasoline.

PORTABLE MASSAGE PARLOR: camper or truck pulling a mobile home (MW).

PORTABLE PARKING LOT: auto carrier (SE).

PORTABLE PIPELINE: gasoline tank truck; milk tanker.

PORTABLE RIG: CB that can be used outside home or car, with its own antenna and battery pack.

PORTABLE ROAD BLOCK: McLean truck.

PORTABLE STOCK YARD: truck carrying cattle.

PORTRAIT PAINTER: police radar (SE).

POSITIVE: yes.

POSITIVE GROUND: the positive battery terminal of a vehicle is connected to the body and frame.

POSITORY: positive; affirmative.

POST: milepost along the expressway.

POST HOLES: empty load.

POSTAGE STAMP: female (NE).

POT HOLE TOWN: Pittsburgh, Pennsylvania.

POTTY MOUTH: one who uses profane or obscene language on the CB (SE).

POUND METER: S-meter.

POUNDS: meter reading in "S" units; e.g. "Thanks for the come back, good buddy. How many pounds am I layin' on you?"

POUR ON THE COAL: accelerate.

POWERHOUSE: strong CB station.

PRE-AMP: power microphone.

PREGNANT ROLLER SKATE: Volkswagen (W).

PREGNANT SKATE BOARD: Volkswagen van (NW).

PREGNANT VW: Pacer (NE).

PRESCRIPTION: FCC regulations.

PRESIDENT'S MEN: Federal government officials (MW).

PRESS SOME SHEETS: sleep (SW); e.g. "I've been on the rip strip too long; it's time to press some sheets."

PRINCE ALBERT TOWN: Port Arthur, Texas (SW).

PROFESSIONAL: trucker.

PULL IN FOR A SHORT, SHORT: restroom stop (SE).

PULL IN THEM REINS: slow down.

PULL SWITCHES: turn off and close down CB rig.

PULL THE BIG ONE: sign-off; turning off the CB (NW).

PULL THE BIG SWITCH: sign-off; turn off the CB set.

PULL YOU OUT: understand what you are saying (can or cannot understand; depends on sentence).

PULL YOUR HAMMER BACK: slow down, police ahead (SW).

PULLING 'EM DOWN: police pulling vehicles to the side of the road.

PULLING THE PLUG: turning off the CB set.

PUMP: linear amplifier.

PUMPKIN: flat tire. Often results from tire ailments.

PUSH WATER: gasoline (SW).

PUSHIN' IT: driving fast.

PUSHING A RIG: driving a truck.

PUSHMOBILE: vehicle moving very slowly; truck with a full load going uphill slowly.

PUSHOLINE: gasoline (SW).

PUT AN EYEBALL ON HIM: look; saw (SE, SW).

PUT AN EYEBALL ON 'YA: see you in person.

PUT IT ON THE FLOOR AND LOOKING FOR SOME MORE: full speed (SE).

PUT ON THE AIR: put on the brakes.

PUT ON THE FEEDBAG: eat a meal; e.g. "We be gone, good buddy, it's time to put on the feedbag."

PUT ON THE IRON: attach chains to the tires.

PUT ONE FOOT ON THE FLOOR, HANG YOUR TOENAILS ON THE RADIATOR AND LET THE MOTOR TOTE 'ER: accelerate.

PUT THE GOOD NUMBERS ON YOU: best wishes (threes and eights).

PUT THE HAMMER DOWN: accelerate.

PUT THE HAMMER IN THE TOOL BOX: slow down.

PUT THE PEDAL TO THE FLOOR: accelerate.

PUT THE PEDAL TO THE METAL: accelerate.

PUT THE PEDAL TO THE METAL AND LET IT ROAR: road is clear, drive desired speed (MW); accelerate.

PUT THE WORD ON THE BASE: mobile unit to a base unit which uses telephone (SE).

PUT YOUR FOOT ON THE FLOOR AND LET THE MOTOR TOTE 'ER: accelerate (SE).

PUT YOUR PEDAL TO THE METAL AND LET YOUR MOTOR TOTE 'ER: accelerate.

PUT YOUR PEDAL TO THE METAL AND HAVE YOURSELF A BALL 'CAUSE IN THAT NORTHBOUND LANE WE HAVEN'T SEEN NOTHIN' AT ALL: the way is clear so drive the desired speed; sign-off.

PUT YOURSELF UP HERE: road is clear of police and obstructions (SE).

PUTTING OUT: sending out a signal (refers to strength of signal); e.g. "How many pounds am I putting out?"

Q-CODE: three-letter combinations beginning with Q (e.g., QRA, QSB, QTO) that represent specific messages. For the complete Q-code, see page 242.

QSL CARD: postcard bearing callsign of other CB operator and used to verify communication or to report reception.

QUAD CITIES: Davenport, Iowa.

QUAD CITY: Moline, Illinois.

QUAIL: desirable girl under the legal age of consent.

QUAKE CITY: San Francisco, California.

QUASAR: girl; woman. Comes from Motorola TV commercial, "works in a drawer."

QUEEN CITY: Cincinnati, Ohio (MW); Springfield, Missouri (MW).

QUICK TRIP AROUND THE HORN: scanning the CB channels.

QUICKIE: short conversation.

QUIET HOURS: FCC-imposed restriction on operating hours of a CB station.

QUIZ: breath test.

R-F: radio frequency.

RACHET JAW or RATCHET JAWER: CBer who hogs the channel; an old-time CBer.

RACHET JAWING: talk; idle talk; talking too long.

RACK: bed; e.g. "I've been on this super slab all day; now it's time to hit the rack."

RADAR ALLEY: Interstate 90 in Ohio.

RADIDIO: CB radio.

RADIO: CB radio.

RADIO CHECK: meter reading; statement of the quality of transmission. Usually asked for by a new CBer who feels left out and wants someone to speak to him.

RAGCHEW: gossip or chit-chat for an extended period.

RAGS: bad tires.

RAIN LOCKER: shower room (W).

RAISE: make contact with a person by CB.

RAKE THE LEAVES: last CB vehicle in a line of two or more; look for police from the rear.

RALLY: intermediate size CB gathering.

RAMBLE ON: move.

RAT RACE: heavy traffic.

REACT: Radio Emergency Associated Citizens Teams; National Headquarters, 111 East Wacker Drive, Chicago, Illinois 60601.

READ: hear.

READING THE MAIL: monitoring.

REBOUND: return trip; e.g. "Have a good day today and a better day tomorrow and we'll catch you on the rebound."

RED-EYE: liquor.

RED WHEEL: red lights on some police cars (MW).

RED, WHITE & BLUES: beer (SW).

REDNECK RADIO: radio transmission using only CB slang terms.

REEFER: refrigerated truck; e.g. "Reefer full of swinging beefs"—sides of beef on the way to market.

RELOCATION CONSULTANTS: moving vans.

REST: Radio Emergency Safety Teams, organized to monitor radio and citizen's radio service frequencies to aid mariners requiring assistance.

REST 'EM UP PLACE: rest area (SE).

REWIND: return trip (NE).

RIDE SHOT GUN: not driving; passenger riding on right side of cab.

RIDER: vehicle without CB following one so equipped (SE).

RIDING THE PONIES: drinking beer (S).

RIG: CB radio and equipment; tractor trailer truck.

RIG GIG: truck-driving job.

RIG RIP-OFF: stolen CB radio.

RINKY DINK: CB radio (SE).

RIOT SQUAD: neighbors who get interference from CB transmissions (NW).

RIP STRIP: expressway.

RIVER CITY: Lawrence, Kansas; Memphis, Tennessee (SE); Paducah, Kentucky (MW); San Antonio, Texas (SW).

RIZZO'S RAIDERS: Philadelphia, Pennsylvania police (NE).

ROACH COACH: garbage truck.

ROAD HOG: driver who drives in more than one lane; driver who straddles two lanes.

ROAD JOCKEY: driver of a tractor trailer.

ROAD TAR: coffee.

ROCK: slang for crystal.

ROCK (THE): Rock Island, Illinois.

ROCK CITY: Little Rock, Arkansas (SE, SW); Chattanooga, Tennessee.

ROCK IT: drive vehicle forward and back repeatedly to free it from mud or snow.

ROCKET CITY: Huntsville, Alabama.

ROCKING CHAIR: middle CB vehicle in a line of three or more.

ROCKY MOUNTAIN KOOL AID: Coors beer.

RODEO TOWN: Cheyenne, Wyoming.

RODGIE: yes; affirmative; I understand (MW).

ROGER: yes; okay; correct; understand?; message received.

ROGER-D: okay; correct; message received.

RODGER-DODGER?: do you understand?; I understand; yes.

ROGER RAMJET: driver exceeding speed limit (MW).

ROGER ROLLER SKATE: driver doing 20 miles over the speed limit (W); e.g. "There goes a roger roller skate, let him get the bear bite."

ROLL AND REST: periodic intervals of driving and stopping to sleep by long-haul driver.

ROLLER SKATE: small car.

ROLLING: moving.

ROLLING BEARS: police on the move (SE).

ROLLING DOMINOES: gamblers (MW).

ROLLING REFINERY: truck hauling gas or oil (SW).

ROLLING ROAD BLOCK: vehicle going under the speed limit and holding up traffic.

ROUNDTABLE: conversation of three or more CB operators whereby each station transmits in turn to the others.

ROVER: police.

RUB EYEBALLS: talk with a CBer in person.

RUBBER CITY: Akron, Ohio (MW).

RUBBER DUCK: lead CB vehicle in a line of two or more watches for police, obstructions. (Term comes from "Convoy" record.)

RUBBER LIPS: one who talks too much.

RUBBERBAND GOING: building speed (SE).

RUBBERNECK: watch women; slow down to look at a break-down or accident.

RUBBERNECKERS: lookers; e.g. "The rubberneckers going past that wreck are causing this four lane parking lot."

RUDE DUDE: reckless or rude driver.

RUG RATS: children (W).

RUMBLE SEAT: CBer on the side in a roundtable conversation, waiting his turn to transmit.

RUN INTERFERENCE: speeding car without CB which police will stop.

RUN OUT THE FRONT END: put the back door (rear CB vehicle) out of range (SE).

RUN THROUGH THE RAINDROPS: take a shower (NE).

RUNNING: putting out power (usually refers to power putput; e.g. "I'm running about 30 watts E.R.P. from this lil' ol' modulator.")

RUNNING A BOOT: using a linear amplifier to boost output (NW).

RUNNING ALLIGATOR STATION: CB channel hog (all mouth and no ears) (S).

RUNNING BAREFOOT: operating CB set legally (in terms of power).

RUNNING BEAR: police on the move.

RUNNING SHOT GUN: driving partner.

RUNNING TOGETHER: CBers staying in contact on the highway (SE).

RUNNING VAN GOGH: vehicle without CB.

S.D.: San Diego, California.

S & H GREEN STAMPS: money.

"S" METER: meter which indicates the level of an intercepted signal and which is calibrated in "S" units. One "S" unit equals 5 decibels (DB). (CBers refer to "S" units as pounds.)

1 "S" unit = faint, barely perceptible signal
2 "S" units = very weak signal
3 "S" units = weak signal
4 "S" units = fair signal
5 "S" units = fairly good signal
6 "S" units = good signal
7 "S" units = moderately strong signal
8 "S" units = strong signal
9 "S" units = extremely strong signal

S-O-S: Secretary of State (of Illinois), official office which licenses motor vehicle operators in Illinois.

S/rf METER: provided on some CB rigs to indicate relative strength of an intercepted signal when receiving and the relative rf power output when transmitting.

S-S-B: single sideband. An AM radio transmission technique in which only one sideband is transmitted. The other one and the carrier are suppressed.

S-W-R: standing wave ratio.

S-W-R METER: a circuit which measures the standing wave ratio at the transceiver end of the antenna transmission line.

SAFE TRUCKIN': drive safely.

SAFER SHAFFER: Shaffer truck.

SAILBOAT FUEL: driving empty; out of gas.

SAILOR CITY: Norfolk, Virginia.

SALT AND PEPPER: police of any kind (MW).

SALT MINES: place of employment.

SALT SHAKER: snowplow with or without sand and salt spreader (NE); sand truck (NE); cinder truck.

SAN QUENTIN: desirable girl under the legal age of consent.

SAN QUENTIN JAIL BAIT: attractive, under-age female hitch-hiker (SE).

SAND BLASTER: salt (or sand) spreading vehicle, used on slippery roads.

SANDBAGGING: police waiting at radar trap and ticketing speeders. e.g. "Smokey's at milemaker 101 sandbagging 'em and passing out green stamps."

SANDBOX: bathroom.

SARDINE CAN: Gremlin automobile (SW).

SAVAGES: CBers who hog the channel.

SAY AGAIN: repeat your transmission.

SAY WHAT?:   what did you say?; repeat message.

SCAB: term ham operators use for CBers.

SCALE CITY: Toledo, Ohio.

SCALE HOUSE: weigh station; e.g. "Bring yourself on up here, the scale house is clean."

SCALE HOUSE IS ALL RIGHT: weigh station is closed.

SCALE HOUSE IS CLEAN: weigh station closed.

SCANNER RECEIVER: one that automatically tunes itself to pre-selected channels, stopping where a signal is heard and resuming scanning when signal is gone.

SCARECROW: parked, empty police vehicle, used as a decoy or to check traffic.

SCATTERSTICK: vertical antenna with a ground plane.

SCHOOL TWENTY: location of school.

SCOFFLAW: FCC rule violator.

SCRATCH THE SANDBOX: go to the restroom (MW).

SCRATCHIN':   vehicle is moving at its best pace.

SCREEN: mirror (rear view or side view).

SCRUB BRUSH: street-cleaning truck.

SEAT COVER: attractive woman or girl; passenger; e.g. "Hey, good buddy, lay an eyeball on that seat cover comin' up in that show-off lane."

SEEING-EYE DOG: device for detecting presence of police radar.

SET IT DOWN: stop quickly.

SET OF DIALS: CB radio.

SET OF DOUBLES: tractor trailer truck.

7-0-8's: beer (SW).

SEVEN THREES: sign-off.

SEVENTEEN-WHEELER: 18-wheeler with flat tire.

SEVENTY-THIRDS TO YOU: sign-off; best wishes.

SEVENTY-THREE: best wishes.

SHACK: room where CB set is installed; railroad conductor.

SHAKE THE BUSHES: lead CB vehicle looking for police, obstructions (NW).

SHAKE THE LEAVES: lead CB vehicle looking for police, obstructions.

SHAKE THE LIGHTS: blink headlights to warn or signal other drivers.

SHAKE THE TREES: lead CB vehicle looking for police, obstructions.

SHAKE THE TREES (or BUSHES) AND RAKE THE LEAVES: front CB vehicle in the group watches ahead for police and obstructions, back vehicle watches behind.

SHAKESPEARE TOWN: Stratford, Connecticut (NE).

SHAKEY CITY: Los Angeles, California.

SHAKEYSIDE: California.

SHAKING IT: moving (SE).

SHAKING THE WINDOWS: clear reception of signal (W).

SHAMUS: policeman.

SHANTY SHAKER: truck delivering mobile home.

SHARK TOWN: Long Island (New York).

SHEEP HERDER: inept driver.

SHIM: to illegally boost power of CB radio.

SHOAT AND GOAT CONDUCTOR: trucker hauling live animals.

SHOES: linear amplifier; illegal piece of gear which increases output to several hundred watts.

SHORT BREAK: short conversation on CB.

SHORT, SHORT: soon; restroom stop.

SHOT AN EYEBALL ON IT: saw it (MW).

SHOT GUN: police radar; e.g. "How about it I-40, we definitely got a bear with a shot gun at Exit 31;" passenger in truck; e.g. "I'm ridin' shot gun on this K-Whomper."

SHOULDER BOULDER: empty, parked vehicle on side of the road.

SHOUT: call for a specific person on the CB set; e.g. "I'm hanging out on channel 13, Sugar Britches, give me a shout tonight."

SHOVE 'ER DOWN AND COME AROUND: you may pass at any desired speed (SW).

SHOVEL COAL: accelerate (SE).

SHOW-OFF LANE: passing lane (SE).

SHY TOWN: Chicago, Illinois (comes from Chi Town).

SICK HORSE: truck that isn't running properly; truck with low power.

SIDE DOOR: passing lane (SE); e.g. "Who we got comin' up on my side door?"

SIDEBANDER: CBer who operates a single sideband CB set (NW).

SIGHTSEER: slow-moving vehicle.

SIN CITY: Cincinnati, Ohio (MW); Las Vegas, Nevada (W); Newport, Kentucky (MW).

SINKING SHIP: vehicle nearly out of fuel.

SIOUX (THE): Sioux Falls, South Dakota.

SISSY SQUAD: two or more male homosexuals (NE).

SITTIN' BY: stop transmitting to allow another CBer to talk; monitoring.

SITTING IN THE SADDLE: middle CB vehicle in a line of three or more (SE).

SITTING UNDER THE LEAVES: hidden police car.

SIX-TEN: make love (NE).

SIX-WHEELER: small truck; passenger car pulling a trailer.

SIXES AND EIGHTS: best wishes.

SKATE JOCKEY: driver of a sports or other high-performance car.

SKATING RINK: slippery road; icy road.

SKINS: tires.

SKIP: radio signal from a distant radio station reflected by the ionosphere.

SKIP SHOOTER: unlicensed CBer (NW); CBer transmitting over the legal wattage; CBer receiving and transmitting over legal limit of 150 miles.

SKIPLAND: distant radio signal.

SKIPPER: CBer transmitting over the legal wattage; CBer who receives and transmits over the 150 mile legal limit.

SKIPTALK: long range signal creating congestion for local CBers; activity of talking with distant CBers.

SKIRT: woman.

SKUNK JUICE: linear amplifier.

SKY BEAR: police helicopter.

SKY MOUNTY: police helicopter.

SKYHOOK: base station antenna, usually over-sized.

SLAMMER: jail (W).

SLAPPERS: windshield wipers.

SLAUGHTER HOUSE: Channel 11 (NW).

SLAVE DRIVERS: CBers who hog channel.

SLED HEAD: snowmobile enthusiast.

SLEEPER: truck that has a sleeping compartment.

SLEEPIN' PEEPERS: vehicle with no headlights on (MW).

SLICK AND CLEAR AS A SPRING DAY: road clear of police and obstructions.

SLICK LIKE SLIME ON A DOORKNOB: icy road (MW); the way is clear.

SLICK TENNIS SHOES: bald tires.

SLIDER: between the channels, as on a sideband radio (NW).

SLIDING MY WHEELS: slowing down or stopping (NW).

SLIP AND SLIDE: slippery road (SE).

SLOP: bad fuel (SE).

SLOPPY JOES: state troopers (SE).

SMILE AND COMB YOUR HAIR: radar ahead (SE, SW); e.g. "Better smile and comb your hair when you go by that mile marker 186."

SMOKE: police.

SMOKE 'EM OUT: exceed the speed limit slightly (not enough to get a ticket) in order to flush hidden police cars out of hiding.

SMOKE 'EM UP BEAR: police of any kind (SE).

SMOKE HIM: pass another vehicle.

SMOKE ON BROTHER: accelerate (SE).

SMOKE (SMOKEY) REPORT: police location report.

SMOKE SIGNALS: police in the area.

SMOKE SCREEN: police radar (SE).

SMOKE SOME DOPE: accelerate (SE); e.g. "You got the green light so smoke some dope if you want to."

SMOKER: police; tractor emitting excessive smoke from exhaust pipe.

SMOKEY: police of any kind.

SMOKEY BEAR: state police.

SMOKEY BEAVER: policewoman (SE).

SMOKEY CHOPPER: police helicopter.

SMOKEY CITY: Pittsburgh, Pennsylvania.

SMOKEY CITY WEST: Cleveland, Ohio.

SMOKEY DOZING: patrol car stopped.

SMOKEY GRAZING GRASS: police car on the median strip.

SMOKEY ON FOUR LEGS: mounted police (used in New York City and Chicago only).

SMOKEY ON RUBBER: policeman moving.

SMOKEY ON THE GROUND: policeman out of the patrol car.

SMOKEY ON THE MOVE: police moving around.

SMOKEY THE BEAR: state police.

SMOKEY TWO-WHEELER: motorcycle police (W).

SMOKEY WITH A CAMERA: police with radar.

SMOKEY WITH EARS: police with CB; e.g. "Talk to the Pig Iron; he's a smokey with ears."

SMOKEY'S OFF THE ROAD, SMOKEY'S IN THE GRASS, SMOKEY'S OUT RAKING LEAVES, BUT WE'VE GOT CB's: sign-off (SE).

SMOKEY'S THICK: police are everywhere (NE).

SMOKING: driving very fast.

SMOKING HABIT: New York State Department of Air Pollution (NE).

SMOKING WITH THE DEVIL: driving unsafely (too quickly for the road conditions).

SMUDGE POT: vehicle (usually a diesel tractor) emitting black smoke from exhaust.

SNAFU: foul-up (abbreviation for Situation Normal, All Fouled Up).

SNAKE: S-curve on road.

SNAKE DEN: fire station (SW).

SNEAKER: CBer with illegal linear amplifier.

SNEAKY SNAKE: hidden patrol car; police with CB set (SE); e.g. "How about you 18-wheelers on this I-55; we got a sneaky snake on the overpass at Exit 22. 10-4?"

SNIPER: hidden radar trap.

SNOOPERS: lights on a marked police car; e.g. "Here comes a Tijuana taxi with its snoopers on."

SNOOPERSCOPE: illegally high antenna.

SNORE SHELF: bed.

SNUFF-DIPPERS: roadside or truckstop prostitutes.

SNUFF SKEETER: friendly term for a person.

SNUFFY SMITH: Smith Transfer Company truck (NE).

SOCKS: linear amplifier to boost CB output.

SODA FOUNTAIN: truck carrying bottled gas.

SOLID STATE: electronic device or circuit employing no tubes.

SOMEONE SPILLED HONEY ON THE ROAD: state troopers ahead everywhere (NW).

SONNET: advertisement for a product over the CB radio (illegal) (NW).

SORE FOOT: flat tire (MW).

SOUNDING CHOICE: clear reception of signal.

SOUP COOLER: mouth.

SOUPED UP: CB modified with illegally high power.

SPACE CITY: Houston, Texas (SW); Huntsville, Alabama (SE).

SPARKIE: electrician (W).

SPEED TOWN: Indianapolis, Indiana.

SPIN OUT: lose traction on a slippery road.

SPITTIN' AND GETTIN': driving very fast (SW).

SPLASHED ON: interrupted on the channel by someone breaking in.

SPLATTER: unintelligible interference on the channel.

SPLIT BEAVER: stripper.

SPOKE TO US: answer back (SE); e.g. "Come on, you got that one and only Sugar Britches, spoke to us."

SPORT CITY: Shreveport, Louisiana (SE).

SPOT THE BODY: park the trailer.

SPREADING THE GREENS: police passing out speeding tickets (SE).

SPRING WATER: beer or liquor (S).

SPUD TOWN: Boise, Idaho.

SPY IN THE SKY: police helicopter (SE); e.g. "We got a spy in the sky at this Exit 182 on this I-40."

SQUASHING THE KEY: activating the mike.

SQUAWK BOX: CB radio.

SQUEEZE-N-EIGHTS: affectionate term meaning kisses between a couple (NE).

SQUELCH: electronic circuit in a receiver which mutes the speaker except when a radio signal is intercepted; cuts out noise between intercepted transmissions.

STACK: exhaust pipe on diesel vehicle.

STACK THEM EIGHTS: best regards.

STAG CITY: Hartford, Connecticut.

STAGE STOP: truck stop (SW).

STALL BALL: traffic tie-up.

STAND BY: wait a while.

STAR CITY: Roanoke, Virginia.

STARVE THE BEARS: don't let the police give you a speeding ticket.

STATE BEAR: state trooper.

STATION LICENSE: in the Citizens Radio Service, a license granted by the FCC to operate any number of transceivers under control of the same license.

STAY BETWEEN THE JUMPS AND BUMPS: drive safely; sign-off.

STAY BETWEEN THE JUMPS AND THE BUMPS AND TRUCK OVER ALL THE HUMPS: drive safely; sign-off.

STEEL CITY (or TOWN): Bethlehem, Pennsylvania; Birmingham, Alabama (SE); Pittsburgh, Pennsylvania; Pueblo, Colorado.

STEPPED ALL OVER YOU: interrupted transmission (SE).

STEPPED ON: interference is coming from another station; conversation interrupted by another CBer.

STEPPED ON THE BEAR'S TOES: broke the law, speed limit, etc. (SE).

STEPPING: moving (SE).

STOP TO GET GROCERIES: stop and eat (SW).

STRAIGHT SHOT: road is clear of police and obstructions (SE); e.g. "You definitely got a straight shot all the way into that Shakey City. Come on!"

STRAPPED FOR TIME: behind schedule.

STRAWBERRY CITY: Portland, Tennessee.

STREAK: move.

STREAKING: full speed (MW); e.g. "Mercy sakes we be doin' it to it in the left lane and we be definitely streaking."

STRIP HER: unload shipment from a truck.

STROKING: flattery.

STROKING YOUR LIZARD: masturbating (SW).

STROLLER: CBer with a walkie-talkie.

STRUT: move.

STRUTTIN': moving.

STUPEN: pretending (SE); e.g. "That bear's not stupen; he's passin' out those green stamps."

SUBSEQUENTLY OR INDIRECTLY WE'LL CATCH YA COME LATELY ON THE FREQUENTLY, 10-4?: sign-off.

SUCK IT UP: drink (usually refers to liquor).

SUCKER: CB set in the repair shop or not working properly.

SUCKER BRAKES: vacuum brakes.

SUDS: beer (W).

SUICIDE CARGO: dangerous cargo.

SUICIDE JOCKEY: trucker hauling explosives.

SUICIDE SLEEPER: truck with a sleeping compartment over the cab.

SUN CITY: El Paso, Texas; Phoenix, Arizona.

SUNBEAM: witty CBer.

SUNOCO: New York State police car (blue and yellow) (NE).

SUNOCO MOBILE: New York State trooper (NE).

SUNOCO SPECIAL: New York State police (NE).

SUPER CHICKEN: truck belonging to Yellow Freight System.

SUPER COLA: beer (S).

SUPER SKATE: highway performance car; Corvette or other sports car.

SUPER SKIRT: girl or woman.

SUPER SLAB: expressway.

SUPER STRUCTURE: bridge.

SUPERBOWL CITY: Pittsburgh, Pennsylvania.

SUPERDOME CITY: New Orleans, Louisiana (SE).

SUPPOSITORY: negative; no (SE).

SWABBY TOWN: San Diego, California.

SWAMPER: person who rides along to help.

SWEEP THE LEAVES: bring up the rear; last CBer in a line of two or more vehicles, watching for police behind.

SWEET LADY: woman.

SWEET THING: female CB operator; female.

SWINDLE SHEET: trucker's log sheet or book.

SWINGING BEEF: frozen sides of meat; beef on hooks inside refrigerated truck.

SYNTHESIZER: device for crystal controlling a large number of frequencies with a few crystals.

T TOWN: Texarkana, Texas and Arkansas (SW).

T-R SWITCH: transmit-receive switch.

T-V-I: television interference from CB sets (abbreviation of Tennessee Valley Indians).

T-X: telephone.

TACO CITY (or TOWN):   El Paso, Texas; San Antonio, Texas.

TACO TOWN: Corpus Christi, Texas.

TAGS: license plates.

TAILBOARD ARTIST: person who believes he drives perfectly.

TAILGATING: driving too closely behind another vehicle.

TAKING PICTURES: police using radar; e.g. "You got a bear in the median at Exit 204 and he's taking pictures for sure. 10-4?"

TAKING PICTURES EACH WAY: two-way police radar.

TALKING CANDLE: person who uses CB to help others.

TALKING SKIP: talking to someone at a great distance, due to radio signal reflected by the ionosphere.

TANKER: tractor trailer carrying liquid.

TAR: coffee.

TATTLETALE: police in helicopter.

TAXI: marked police car (short for Tijuana taxi).

TEAR JERKER: CBer who tells sad stories on the radio.

TEDDY BEAR: state trooper.

TEN BYE-BYE: sign-off.

TEN-CODE: abbreviations originally used by police and other land mobiles, now widely used by CBers; used to minimize the use of air time. For complete ten-codes ('Official' and Abbreviated) see pages 239-242.

TEN-FER: affirmative; yes; thanks.

TEN-FORTY: message received.

TEN-FOUR: hello; positive; yes; O.K.; I understand; do you understand?; what?; definitely; e.g. "A big ten-four to that, good buddy." Ten-four is the most widely and frequently used term in CB slanguage.

TEN-HUNDRED ROOM: restroom; bathroom.

TEN-ONE HUNDRED (10-100): restroom stop (SW, W).

TEN-ONE THOUSAND (10-1000): FCC representative (W); homosexual (NE).

TEN-POUNDER: excellent reception.

TEN-ROGER: message received; do you understand?

TEN-TEN: through transmitting but monitoring.

TEN-TEN AND LISTNIN' IN: transmission is complete and I'm monitoring.

TEN-TEN 'TIL WE DO IT AGAIN: sign-off.

TEN-THIRTY-FOUR (10-34): emergency.

TEN-TWO THOUSAND (10-2000): dope pusher (W).

TENNESSEE SLICK STICKS: Neutronics Hustler Phased Antennas; dual antennas.

TENNESSEE VALLEY INDIANS: interference on television caused by CB transmission (abbreviated T-V-I).

TENNIS SHOES: truck tires.

TENSE: heavy traffic.

TERRIBLE SITUATION: describes Channel 1 when sidebanders are talking on it (MW).

TEXAS STRAWBERRIES: shelled corn (SW).

TEXAS TRUNK: vehicle carrying hidden, illegal linear amplifier.

THAT'S A COPY: message received.

THE MAN: an official (police, government, or company).

THERMOS BOTTLE: milk tanker; gasoline tank truck.

THIN: very weak radio signal (NW).

THIN MAN: CBer whose radio gives out a very weak signal (NW).

THIRD RAILER: vehicle straddling center divider after an accident (NE).

THIRTY-THREE: emergency (stands for 10-33, 'Official' 10-Code).

THIRTY-TWELVE: sign-off; best wishes (ten-four three times).

THIRTY WEIGHT: coffee (SW).

THREE-FIVE: masturbate (NE).

THREE-FIVING THE MIKE: keying and unkeying the mike rapidly. (NE).

THREE-LEGGED BEAVER: male homosexual.

THREE-LEGGED FOUR-WHEELER: broken-down car (SE).

THREES: short for 73's which is a salutation; it can mean hello, goodbye or best wishes; e.g. "I'll say threes, Sugar Britches."

THREES AND EIGHTS: sign-off; best wishes (SW).

THREES AND NINES: best wishes.

THREES ON YOU: best regards.

THROW A SHOE: get a flat tire.

THUNDER CHICKEN: Ford Thunderbird (SE).

THUNDERSTICKS: 9-foot whip antennas (MW).

TICKS: minutes (NE).

TIE THE RIBBONS: end the conversation.

TIED UP: slowed or stopped by obstruction on the road.

TIGER IN A TANK: linear amplifier to boost CB output.

TIGER IN THE TANK: driver who disregards safety rules and drives discourteously (MW).

TIGHTEN UP ON THE RUBBERBAND: accelerate (SE).

TIGHTEN YOUR SEAT DOWN, WE'RE RUNNING HEAVY: we are accelerating to full speed (SE).

TIJUANA TAXI: police; wrecker (MW); an official vehicle showing lots of lights and markings.

TIME ON THE DIME: estimated time of arrival at destination.

TIN CAN: CB radio.

TINSEL CITY (or TOWN): Hollywood, California (W).

TITLE TOWN: Green Bay, Wisconsin.

TOBACCO CAPITOL: Springfield, Tennessee.

TOBACCO CITY: Winston-Salem, North Carolina.

TOENAILS ARE SCRATCHING: full speed (SE).

TOENAILS IN THE RADIATOR: full speed (SE).

TOENAILS ON THE FRONT BUMPER: full speed (SE).

TOGA TOWN: Saratoga, New York.

TOILET MOUTH: one who uses profane or obscene language on the CB (W).

TOILET TONGUE: one who uses profane or obscene language on the CB (SW).

TOMATO TOWN: Reynoldsburg, Ohio (MW).

TONKER TOY: CB radio (NE).

TOOLED UP: CB set that has been modified to boost output (NW).

TOOLING ALONG: driving at normal speed.

TOOTHACHE: need new tubes in your radio (S).

TOOTHPICKS: telephone poles (MW).

TOP OF THE WORLD: top of the Edison Bridge (Perth Amboy, New Jersey) (NE).

TOP TWENTY: national CB jamboree held three days each year in a different city.

TOSS THE HAMMER BACK IN THE OL' TOOLBOX: slow down, police ahead (SE).

TRACTOR: truck without a trailer.

TRADING STAMPS: money; e.g. "I got a pocket full of trading stamps and I'm free to spend 'em."

TRAILER TRUCK IT: drive your vehicle.

TRAILER TRUCKING: 18-wheeler's term for driving his rig.

TRAIN STATION: traffic court that fines nearly everybody.

TRAINING WHEELS: learner's permit.

TRAMPLED: conversation blocked out by interference, usually caused deliberately.

TRAMPOLINE: bed.

TRANSCEIVER: combination radio transmitter and receiver.

TRANSMISSION LINE: the coaxial cable that is used to connect the transceiver to the antenna on CB rigs.

TRANSPORTER: truck.

TRASH TOWN: San Angelo, Texas (SW).

TRICK BABE: prostitute (SW).

TRICKY DICK'S: San Clemente, California (W).

TRICYCLE MOTOR: child (SW).

TRIP: how well message is transmitting; e.g. "How are we making the trip?"; strong CB signal heard from a distance.

TROUSERS AND SKIRTS: bi-sexual.

TRUCK 'EM EASY: drive safely; e.g. "You truck 'em easy now and don't let those smokeys get in your britches."

TRUCK 'EM LIGHT: drive safely (SE).

TRUCK 'EM UP STOP: truck stop.

TRUCK FORWARD: move on.

TRUCK JOCKEY: truck driver.

TRUCK ON: move on.

TRUCK STOP ANNIES: prostitutes.

TRUCK STOP COMMANDO: trucker.

TRUCK STOP WAITRESS: prostitute (NE).

TRUCKIN' GUY: fellow truck driver (NE, MW).

TRUCKIN' TEENAGER: teenage hitchhiker.

TRUCKLOADS OF 88's: lots of kisses (NE).

TUNED UP: radio putting out more than the four-watt legal maximum.

TUNNEL OF LOVE: road where conditions or obstructions cause interference with CB reception.

TURKEY: term for CBer, implying either animosity or affection; dumb person (W).

TURKEY AREA: rest area.

TURN-AROUND: round trip, made by a truck leaving and returning to the same terminal.

TURN OVER: stop; e.g. "We'll turn over at that Exit 204."

TURN TWENTY: location of exit or turn.

TURNING MY HOUSE AROUND: turning the antenna for better reception (W).

TURTLE: slow-moving vehicle (NE); camper (SE).

TWELVES: company present (SW).

TWENTY: location; e.g. "What's your twenty now, good buddy?"

TWIN CITIES: Minneapolis/St. Paul, Minnesota.

TWIN CITY: Fort Worth, Texas; Minneapolis, Minnesota; Winston-Salem, North Carolina.

TWIN FORT: Superior, Wisconsin.

TWIN FORTS: Duluth, Minnesota.

TWIN HUSKIES: dual antennas (SE, SW, W).

TWIN MAMAS: dual 9-foot antennas.

TWINS: dual antennas.

TWISTED PAIR: telephone.

TWISTER: highway cloverleaf; interchange.

TWO MILES OF DITCHES FOR EVERY MILE OF ROAD, KEEP YOUR RIG IN THE MIDDLE: drive safely; sign-off.

TWO-STOOL BEAVER: very fat woman.

225 SALE: buying or selling of stolen CB radio or other audio equipment.

TWO-WAY RADAR: radar unit in a moving police car.

TWO-WHEELER: motorcycle.

UCBTA: United CB Truckers Association, P.O. Box 2676, Garland, Texas 75041.

U-S-B: upper sideband.

UNCLE CHARLEY: FCC representative; e.g. "Uncle Charley has gone fox hunting in that Circle City tonight."

UNGOWA BWANA: okay (NW).

UNIT: CB radio; car; truck; one of the transceivers covered by a CB station license when more than one transceiver is used.

USCRC: United States Citizens Radio Council, 3600 Noble, Anniston, Alabama 36201.

USE THE JAKE: slow down (SW); e.g. "You 18-wheelers on that eastbound side better use the jake, we've got some slick spots through here."

V-8 JUICE: gas (SW).

VAN: tractor.

VIRGINIA VITAMIN: pep pill (SW).

VITAMIN A: milk (NE).

VOICE CHECK: radio check.

VOLUNTEER STATE: Tennessee.

VOX: abbreviation for Voice-Operated Relay; device that automatically activates transmitter when CBer speaks into the microphone.

W.T.: walkie-talkie (NE).

WAGGIN' TAIL: camper.

WAGON TRAIN: parade (MW).

WALKED ALL OVER: overpowered by stronger signal; interrupted on channel by someone breaking in.

WALKED ON: overpowered by stronger signal; interrupted on channel by someone breaking in.

WALKIE-T: walkie-talkie.

WALKIE-TALKIE: portable transceiver.

WALKIN': driving.

WALKING IN HERE BLOWING SMOKE: clear reception of signal (SE).

WALKING ON YOU: covering up your signal; e.g. "Come back on that, guy, they're walking on you."

WALKING THE DOG: speaking on the CB over a long distance; clear reception of signal.

WALKING WITH BOOTS: using a linear amplifier.

WALL TO WALL: getting good signal on the CB.

WALL-TO-WALL AND TREE TOP TALL: clear reception of signal (W).

WALL-TO-WALL BEARS: police are everywhere; radar set-up or road block (NE).

WALL-TO-WALL, TEN FEET TALL: clear reception of signal (SE).

WALLACE LANE: middle lane of a three-lane highway.

WALLACE STATE: Alabama.

WALLPAPER: QSL card (NW).

WARDEN: wife.

WASHBOARD: bumpy road.

WASSAHOPS?: what's happening on this channel?

WATCH THE PAVEMENT: drive safely (SE).

WATCH YOUR DONKEY: watch for police coming up from behind (NW); e.g. "You shake the leaves, and I'll watch your donkey for you."

WATER BARREL: Niagara Falls, New York.

WATER HOLE: truck stop (SW); any rest stop.

WATERGATE CITY (or TOWN): Washington, D.C.

WAVE MAKER: water bed.

WAY IS BUENO: road is clear of police and obstructions (SW).

WE: I (used instead of first person singular); e.g. "We be at mile marker 112 and we see a smokey in a plain brown wrapper."

WE BE TOPPIN' THESE HILLS AND POPPIN' THESE PILLS: truckers' sign-off.

WE DOWN, WE GONE, BYE-BYE: sign-off.

WE GO: through transmitting; sign-off.

WE GO BYE-BYE: sign-off (MW).

WE GONE: sign-off; stopping transmitting; through transmitting but monitoring.

WE QUIT: sign-off.

WE UP, WE DOWN, WE CLEAR, WE GONE: sign-off.

WE UP, WE DOWN, WE OUT, WE GONE: sign-off.

WE WENT: sign-off.

WEARING SOCKS: using a linear amplifier to boost CB output.

WEEK-END WARRIORS: National Guard.

WEIGHT MAN: weigh station worker.

WEIGHT WATCHER: weigh station worker (W).

WELFARE STATION: CB purchased with welfare money (W).

WE'LL BE DOIN' IT THE OTHER WAY: we're headed in the opposite direction from you.

WE'RE BACKING 'EM UP NOW: sign-off; slow down (SE).

WE'RE CLEAR: sign-off; road is clear of police and obstructions; e.g. "The one Sugar Britches, KXI-7248, we're clear."

WE'RE DOWN: sign-off (SE).

WE'RE DOWN, OUT, ON THE SIDE: through transmitting but listening (SE).

WE'RE LISTENING: answer back (SE); e.g. "What about that Triple Six one time, we're listening."

WE'RE LOOKING: answer back (SE).

WE'RE OUT: clear of police and obstructions; sign-off.

WE'RE OUT OF IT: clear of police and obstructions; sign-off.

WE'RE TRYING: distant attempt for CB contact.

*WEST*BOUND AND JUST LOOKIN' AROUND: sign-off.

WEST COAST TURNAROUNDS: "bennies"; pep pills (NE, SW).

WESTERN-STYLE COFFEE: day-old coffee.

WHACKEY TOBACKEY: marijuana (SW).

WHAT ABOUT THAT (*handle*)?: call for a specific CBer.

WHAT ABOUT YOU?: call for a specific CBer.

WHAT AM I PUTTING ON YOU?: request for meter reading; desire to know signal strength.

WHAT ARE YOU PUSHING?: what are you driving?

WHAT KIND OF COPY?: request for meter reading; desire to know strength and clarity of signal.

WHATEVERS: state troopers.

WHAT'S YOUR EIGHTEEN?: what kind of truck are you driving?

WHAT'S YOUR HANDLE?: what's your CB code name?

WHAT'S YOUR TWENTY?: request for location.

WHEELING AROUND: driving around.

WHEELS: CB set installed in a vehicle.

WHEN DID YOU GET IN THIS BUSINESS?: how long have you had a CB? (SE).

WHERE DO YOU GET YOUR GREEN STAMPS?: where do you work?

WHIMP: man with little personality or courage (NW).

WHIP: rod for mobile antenna.

WHISKEY STATE: Kentucky.

WHITE KNIGHT: state trooper (from record title).

WHITE RABBIT: policeman.

WHITE RABBIT WITH EARS: police with CB.

WHO DO YOU PULL FOR?: who do you work for? (SE).

WHOMPING ON YOU: interrupting transmission (SE); e.g. "Come back on that, good buddy, somebody's whomping on you."

WIDE SIDE: empty lane on the left.

WILCO: I will comply; okay.

WILLY WEAVER: drunk driver.

WIND CITY: Chicago, Illinois.

WINDJAMMERS: long-winded CBers (NE).

WINDMILL CITY: Nederland, Texas (SW).

WINDOW SHOPPING: looking at pretty girls for dates (NE).

WINDOW WASHER: rainstorm.

WINDY CITY: Chicago, Illinois; Fargo, North Dakota.

WINKIN' BLINKIN': school bus (MW).

WIPE THE BUGS OFF YOUR PLATES: last vehicle with CB in a line watching for police (same as BACK DOOR); e.g. "You watch the front door and we'll wipe the bugs off your plates."

WIPE THE MIRROR: restroom stop.

WIPE THE WINDSHIELD: restroom stop.

WIPED OUT: CB transmission overpowered by a stronger signal.

WOBBLY BOX: mobile home pulled on a flatbed trailer.

WOOD BUTCHER: carpenter (W).

WOODCHUCK: trucker who has low seniority.

WOODPECKER: carpenter (SE).

WOOLY BEAR: woman (SE).

WOOLY CRITTER: good-looking female.

WOOLY-WOOLY: woman (SE).

WORK TWENTY: place of employment.

WORKING FOR THE MOONLIGHT EX-PRESS: driving on back roads at night to avoid weigh stations.

WORKING MAN: truck driver (MW).

WRAP IT UP AND TAKE IT BACK: after your sign-off, we'll be through talking.

WRAPPER: unmarked police car; can be used to refer to car color; e.g. "Hey there on that southbound side, you've got a white wrapper in your lane at mile post 269. 10-4?"

WRINKLE: uneven transmission (SE).

X: ex-wife; ex-husband.

X-L: unmarried woman (W); young lady.

X-Y: spouse.

X-Y-D: daughter.

X-Y-L: wife (stands for ex-young lady); husband (MW); spouse.

X-Y-M: husband.

X-Y-N: male (SW).

X-Y-O: spouse (NW).

X-BAND: radar frequency used by the police.

X-RAY MACHINE: police radar; e.g. "Smokey's got his X-ray machine working at Exit 15."

X-RAYING: trooper with radar.

XEROX?: do you hear me? (SE).

Y-F: wife.

Y-L: young lady.

YAP: conversation on CB.

YELLOW AIR: Gary, Indiana.

YELLOW BREATH: Gary, Indiana.

YELLOWSTONE PARK: congregation of state troopers; road block or radar with several chase cars (NW, SE).

YO: yes (SE).

YO YO: vehicle varying speed (SE).

YOO: yes.

YOU BROKE IT, FIX IT: give a break on the CB, let someone else have the channel (SE).

YOU GOT IT: answer back (MW); permission to speak on channel.

YOU GOTTA COPY ON ME?: do you hear me?

YOUNGVILLE: young children are on channel (NW).

YOUR TELEPHONE IS RINGING: call for specific CBer (SE); e.g. "How about that Mr. McGoo one time. Your telephone is ringing."

YOUR TORN: your turn on the channel (MW).

YOU'RE LOOKING GOOD: clear reception of signal (SE).

YOU'RE NOT THE ONLY ONE ON THE ROAD: police in the area (MW).

ZAPPED: overloaded from a passing vehicle using a powerful linear amplifier at close range, damaging the receiver section of a CB.

ZEPHYR HAUL: shipment of lightweight freight.

Z's: sleep.

Z's-VILLE: sleeping (NE).

ZOO: police station.

CROSS-REFERENCE

A-M CAR RADIO
    baseball radio (MW)

ACCELERATOR PEDAL
    boot rest
    hammer

ACCIDENT (see TRAFFIC ACCIDENT)

ADDRESS (see HOME)

AFFIRMATIVE (see YES)

AIRPLANE
    oversized 'skeeter

AKRON, OHIO
    Rubber City (MW)

ALABAMA
    George Wallace Country (SE)
    Wallace State

ALLENTOWN, PENNSYLVANIA
    Mack City

AMARILLO, TEXAS
    Big A (SW)

AMBULANCE (see also HELP)
    band-aid (NE)
    blood box
    bone box
    emergency vehicle
    meat wagon (W)
    one-way camper

ANCHORAGE, ALASKA
    The Iceberg

ANSWER BACK (see CB CONVERSATION)

ANTENNA (see CB RADIO AND EQUIPMENT)

ARIZONA
Desert State

ARKANSAS
Hog Country (SE)

ATLANTA, GEORGIA
Big A (SE)
Big South
Hot Lanta (SE)
Hot Town (SE)

ATLANTIC CITY, NEW JERSEY
The Boardwalk

ATTACH CHAINS TO TIRES
put on the iron

AUTOMOBILE (see CAR)

AUTOMOBILE GRAVEYARD
boneyard

BALTIMORE, MARYLAND
B.W.
Bal City
Hole in the Wall

BASE STATION (see CB RADIO AND EQUIP-
MENT)

BATON ROUGE, LOUISIANA
B.R. Town

BATTERY TERMINAL
(NEGATIVE)
negative ground

BATTERY TERMINAL *(continued)*

(POSITIVE)
positive ground

BED (see SLEEP)

BEER
barley pop (NW)
brew
brown bottle
buttermilk (SE)
cold coffee (SE)
Colorado Kool Aid (SW)
8-0-7
forty weight (SW)
honey (SE)
Kool Aid (SE, SW)
little pony
red, white & blues (SW)
Rocky Mountain Kool Aid (Coors)
7-0-8's (SW)
spring water (S)
super cola (S)

(DRINKING BEER)
riding the ponies

BEST WISHES (see also DRIVE SAFELY; SIGN-OFF)
big eights
big threes
eights
eights and other good numbers
eighty-eights around the house
fleas on 'ya (NE)
good numbers
good pair

BEST WISHES *(continued)*
>happy numbers
>keep stroking (NE)
>magic numbers on you
>pass the numbers to you
>put the good numbers on you
>seventy-thirds to you
>seventy-three
>sixes and eights
>stack them eights
>thirty-twelve
>threes
>threes and eights (SW)
>threes and nines
>threes on you

BETHLEHEM, PENNSYLVANIA
>Steel City (or Town)

BICYCLE RIDER
>pedal pusher (NE)

BILLINGS, MONTANA
>Big Sky

BINDERS ON FLATBED TRAILER
>boomers

BIRMINGHAM, ALABAMA
>B Town (SE)
>Big B (SE)
>Magic City
>Steel City (SE)

BI-SEXUAL
>trousers and skirts

BOISE, IDAHO
>Spud Town

BOSTON, MASSACHUSETTS
Bean Town (NE)

BOWLING
gutter balling (W)

BOWLING GREEN, KENTUCKY
B.G. Town

BRAKES
binders
sucker brakes (vacuum brakes)

BREAK INTO A CHANNEL (see CB CONVERSA-TION)

BREATH TEST
quiz

BRIDGE
erector set (NE)
super structure

(BRIDGE WITH HIGH CLEARANCE)
high rise

(BRIDGE WITH LOW CLEARANCE)
haircut palace (MW)

BROKE THE LAW OR SPEED LIMIT (see also TICKET)
stepped on the bear's toes (SE)

BUFFALO, NEW YORK
The Buffer

BUS

(GREYHOUND BUS)
big dog

(SCHOOL BUS)
blinkin' winkin'
kiddie can (SE)

(SCHOOL BUS—*continued*)
kiddie car (SE)
winkin' blinkin' (MW)

BUSY
10-6 (Abbreviated 10-Code)

(ARE YOU BUSY?)
QRL

BUTTE, MONTANA
Big Butte

CB AIRWAVES
CB Land

CB ASSOCIATIONS AND ORGANIZATIONS (see
dictionary for addresses)
ALERT
CRW
NCCRA
REACT
REST
UCBTA
USCRC

CB COMMUNICATIONS

(ANYTHING FOR US?)
10-18 ('Official' 10-Code)

(ARE YOU READY?)
QRV

(CAN YOU COMMUNICATE WITH _____?)
QSO

(CAN YOU CONTACT _____?)
10-25 ('Official' 10-Code)

(DO YOU HAVE NEWS OF _____?)
QUA

(LIST OF CB CONVERSATIONS)
log

(POSTCARD)
QSL card

(SHALL I STAND GUARD FOR YOU ON (#)
MHz/KHz?)
QTV

(WHAT IS NEXT MESSAGE NUMBER?)
10-60 ('Official' 10-Code)

(WHAT'S HAPPENING ON THIS CHANNEL?)
Wassahops?

(WILL YOU WAIT?)
QRX

CB CONVERSATION (see also CB USE;
  MESSAGE; SIGN-OFF; TRANSMIT)
    convac (SE)
    jawjacking (MW)
    modjitate
    modulating
    modulation
    rachet jawing
    yap

    (ANSWER BACK; ANSWERING BACK)
    back
    back at 'cha
    back at you
    back to you
    bring it back (SE)
    bring it on
    bring yourself on in (SE)
    come back
    come here
    come on

(ANSWER BACK—*continued*)
come on breaker
do it to me (SE)
give me a shot
give me a shout
give me a shout, shout
go back to him
hit me one time
spoke to us (SE)
we're listening
we're looking (SE)
you got it (MW)

(CALL FOR A SPECIFIC CBer)
break for (*handle*)
calling for
collect call
holler
How about that (*handle*) one time? (SE)
How about you (*handle*)?
long distance telephone is ringing (SE)
shout
your telephone is ringing (SE)
What about that (*handle*)?
What about you?

(CALL FOR ANYONE ON CHANNEL)
give me a shot (SE)
give me a shout (or shout, shout) (SE)
grab bag (NE)

(CONVERSATION INTERRUPTED BY SOME-
ONE BREAKING IN)
splashed on
stepped on
walked all over
walked on

(CONVERSATION OF THREE OR MORE CBers TRANSMITTING IN TURN)
roundtable

(CONVERSATION USING ONLY CB SLANG)
redneck radio

(FIVE MINUTE CONVERSATION LIMIT SET BY FCC)
nickel's worth (MW)

(GIVE PERMISSION TO SPEAK ON CHANNEL)
dump 'er in
go ahead
go break 10 (*or other channel #*)
go breaker
gourd head (MW)
you got it (MW)
your torn (MW)

(MAKE SMALL TALK; GOSSIP)
chew the fat
chit chat
hamming
rachet jaw
ragchew

(OVERHEARD CONVERSATION)
mail

(REQUEST FOR CBer TO END THE CONVERSATION)
clear after you
package 'er up
tie the ribbons
wrap it up and take it back

(REQUEST FOR CBer TO STOP TRANSMITTING AND ALLOW OTHERS TO SPEAK)
boot 'er over
drag your feet

(STOP TRANSMITTING—*continued*)
drop carrier
lay down
let the channel roll
you broke it, fix it (SE)

(REQUEST FOR CBer TO TALK CLOSER TO MIKE)
10-91 ('Official' 10-Code)

(REQUEST FOR SHORT CONVERSATION)
gimme five

(REQUEST PERMISSION TO SPEAK ON CHANNEL)
break
break, break
break channel # (*FCC callsign*)
break (*direction*)bound 18-wheeler
break *10* (*or other channel #*)
breaker broke
breaker busted
CQ
how about an *east*bound (*or other direction*)
10-50 ('Official' 10-Code)

(RETURNING TO CHANNEL SHORTLY)
back in a short, short

(SHALL I STOP TRANSMITTING?)
QRT

(SHORT CONVERSATION)
one time
quickie
short break

(TALK TO HIM AGAIN)
go back to him

(TALK TO YOU LATER)
catch you come later (SW)

(TELL ME)
lay it on me

(TIME IS UP FOR CONTACT)
our nickel is up
10-29 ('Official' 10-Code)

(TURN THE CHANNEL OVER)
kick

CB GATHERING (see also MEET)
coffee break
confab
jamboree
rally

(CB CLUB MEMBERS)
chain gang (NW)

(JAMBOREE SEASON)
J trail

(NATIONAL JAMBOREE)
mothball
top twenty

CB OPERATOR (see also PERSON)
dip stick
good buddy
gunnybegger (MW)
henchmen (group of CBers) (NW)
turkey

(CBer NOT ON USUAL CHANNEL)
fugitive

(CBer WHO DIRECTS CHANNEL TRAFFIC)
channel control

(CBer WHO GIVES OUT MANY QSL CARDS)
paperhanger

(CBer WHO HOGS THE CHANNEL; LONG-WINDED CBer)
alligator
alligator station
cartel (group of CBers) (NW)
channel clown hog (MW)
channel hogger
diarrhea of the mouth (W)
goon squad (group of CBers) (NE)
hag feast (female CBers) (NE)
hagfest (female CBers)
motor mouth
ocean mouth (NE)
rachet jaw
rubber lips
running alligator station
savages
slave drivers
windjammers (NE)

(CBer WHO IS LISTENING)
back seat
bench
better half (MW)
dressed for the ball

(CBer WHO KEYS MIKE WITHOUT SPEAKING)
buttonpusher
carrier
carrier thrower

(CBer WHO OPERATES SINGLE SIDEBAND CB SET)
sidebander (NW)

(CBer WHO TELLS SAD STORIES)
tear jerker

(CBer WHO TRANSMITS ILLEGALLY) (see also CB RADIO AND EQUIPMENT)
apple
flake
skip shooter
skipper
sneaker

(CBer WHO USES D-104 TYPE MICROPHONE)
chicken choker

(CBer WITH SEXY VOICE)
foxy jaws

(CBer WITH WEAK RADIO)
thin man (NW)

(CBers KNOWN NATIONALLY)
glory roll (NW)

(CHANNEL-HOPPING CBer)
fingers

(CHILDREN ON THE CHANNEL)
youngville

(CODE NAME OF CBer)
handle

(DUMB CBer)
ding-a-ling

(EXPERIENCED CBer)
apple
B-T-O (NE)
boast toastie (NW)
rachet jaw

(FEMALE CBer)
dixie cup
lady breaker
sweet thing

(HAM RADIO OPERATOR'S TERM FOR CBer)
scab

(IDLE TALKER; GOSSIP)
bucket mouth
bull jockey

(INEPT RADIO OPERATOR)
appliance operator
lid

(INTERESTING CBer)
fog lifter

(INEXPERIENCED OR BEGINNING CBer)
green apple

(LATE NIGHT TALKERS IN NASHVILLE)
bozos (SE)

(LEGAL OPERATOR)
legal beagle (W)

(LOCAL CBers)
natives

(LOUD CBer)
linear lungs (NW)

(NERVOUS CBer)
cradle baby (NE)

(OBSCENE OR PROFANE TALKER)
bucket mouth
garbage mouth (NE)
latrine lips (W)
potty mouth (SE)
toilet mouth (W)
toilet tongue (SW)

(ONE OF A GROUP ON CB RADIO)
rumble seat

(OPERATOR OF BASE OR FIELD STATION)
anchored modulator

(OPERATOR WHO HELPS OTHERS OVER CB)
talking candle

(OPERATOR WITH "WALKIE-TALKIE" CB)
stroller

(TEENAGE CBer)
bubblegummer

(UNLICENSED CBer)
bootlegger
skip shooter (NW)

(WITTY CBer)
sunbeam

CB RADIO AND EQUIPMENT
beast
box (SE)
CB
chicken box
ears
hillbilly opera house
Japanese toy
lil' ol' modulator
magic metal box
mobile
radidio
radio
rig
rinky dink (SE)
set of dials
squawk box
tin can
tonker toy (NE)
transceiver
unit

(ADDITIONAL RADIO TO SCAN POLICE CHANNELS)
other radio (NW)

(ANTENNA)
hustler

(ANTENNA — BASE STATION, OVERSIZED)
skyhook

(ANTENNA — DIRECTIONAL)
beam
omnidirectional antenna

(ANTENNA — ILLEGALLY HIGH)
snooperscope

(ANTENNA — LONG MOBILE)
big mama
thundersticks (MW)
twin mamas (dual)
whip

(ANTENNA — ROOF MOUNTED)
chrome dome

(ANTENNA — SHORT)
choptop
chopped top (NE)
little mama

(ANTENNA — SWAYING IN THE WIND)
ballet dancer (NE)

(ANTENNA — VERTICAL WITH A GROUND PLANE)
scatterstick

(ANTENNAS — DUAL)
ears
fishing pole and a partner
Tennesse slick sticks (often Neutronics Hustler
  Phased Antennas)

(ANTENNAS—*continued*)
twin huskies (SE, SW, W)
twin mamas (9-foot antennas)
twins

(BASE STATION WITH MANY ANTENNAS)
antenna farm

(BRAND NEW CB)
blessed event (NW)

(CB ACCESSORIES)
goodies (NW)

(CB AT FIXED LOCATION)
base rig
base station
fixed station

(CB CONTROLS)
delta tune
keyboard

(CB IN THE REPAIR SHOP OR NOT WORKING
PROPERLY)
beast (NE)
ear ache (antenna problems)
sucker
toothache (needs new tubes)

(CB INSTALLED IN VEHICLE)
mobile rig
mobile unit
portable rig
wheels

(CB NOT MODIFIED)
barefoot
barefoot mobile
clean cut (NW)

(CB PURCHASED WITH WELFARE MONEY)
welfare station (W)

(CB RADIO THAT MONITORS BUT DOESN'T TRANSMIT)
crocodile station (MW)

(CB RADIO THAT TRANSMITS BUT DOESN'T RECEIVE)
alligator station

(CB WITH ILLEGAL ADDED POWER)
peaked up
souped up
tooled up (NW)
tuned up

(CB WITH LOW POWER)
peanut whistle

(COAXIAL CABLE)
co-ax
transmission line

(CONVERTER THAT MONITORS CB CONVERSATIONS THROUGH AM RADIO)
bear buster

(DEVICE TO REDUCE NOISE ON CB)
A-N-L
noise blanker
noise limiter
squelch

(FREQUENCY CONTROLS)
crystal
frequency synthesizer
rock
synthesizer

(LINEAR AMPLIFIER) (illegal)
after burner
black box
boots
feet

(LINEAR AMPLIFIER—*continued*)

foot warmer
galoshes
hamburger helper (W)
heater
hot foot (NW)
kicker
linear
little foot warmer
little help
moccasins
persuader
pump
shoes
skunk
socks
tiger in a tank

(MICROPHONE)
lollipop
mike
pre-amp

(MICROPHONE CIRCUIT MODIFIER)
modulation booster

(MICROPHONE/EARPHONE IN ONE UNIT)
handset

(PORTABLE CB WITH OWN BATTERY)
handie-talkie
W.T. (NE)
Walkie-T
walkie-talkie

(PRINTED CIRCUIT)
P-C

(PUSH-TO-TALK SWITCH)
P-T-T switch

(RECEIVER — AUTOMATIC TUNING)
scanner receiver

(STANDING WAVE RATIO)
S-W-R

(STOLEN CB)
rig rip-off

(STRONG CB STATION)
powerhouse

(TRANSCEIVER — SMALL, HAND-HELD)
brick

(TRANSMIT-RECEIVE SWITCH)
T-R switch

(TUBELESS ELECTRONICS)
solid state

(VOICE-OPERATED RELAY)
VOX

CB REPAIRMAN NEEDED
10-89 ('Official' 10-Code)

CB USE

(ADVERTISEMENT ON CB) (illegal)
sonnet (NW)

(CB RADIO NOT IN USE)
in the pen

(DURING WHAT HOURS IS YOUR STATION OPEN?)
QTU

(HOW LONG HAVE YOU HAD A CB?)
When did you get in this business?

(LEGAL USE)
ears on
running barefoot

(MOBILE TO BASE USING TELEPHONE)
put the word on the base (SE)

(OPERATE ILLEGALLY WITH LINEAR
AMPLIFIER (see also CB RADIO AND EQUIP-
MENT — LINEAR AMPLIFIER)
boots on (MW)
high gear
running a boot
shim
walking with boots
wearing socks

(TRANSMIT WITHOUT A LICENSE)
bootleg

(USE SOMEONE ELSE'S CB)
bootleg (W)

(USING A D-104 TYPE MICROPHONE)
choking a chicken

(WILL YOU KEEP YOUR STATION OPEN FOR
FURTHER COMMUNICATION?)
QTX

CALIFORNIA
Shakeyside

CAMPER (see VAN)

CANADIAN *GENERAL RADIO SERVICE*
GRS

CANTON, OHIO
Fame Town

CAR (see also LAW ENFORCEMENT VEHICLE;
VEHICLE)
four-wheeler
mobile
unit

(AMC CAR)
Kenosha Cadillac

(CAR BROKEN DOWN)
third railer (NE)
three-legged four-wheeler (SE)

(CAR PULLING A CAMPER)
mobile mattress

(CAR PULLING A TRAILER)
piggy back
six-wheeler

(CHEVROLET)
Detroit vibrator

(FORD MUSTANG OR COLT)
horse (SE, SW)

(FORD THUNDERBIRD)
bird
Thunder Chicken (SE)

(GREMLIN)
beach ball buggy (SW)
sardine can (SW)

(PACER)
pregnant VW (NE)

(PLYMOUTH BARRACUDA)
fish (SE)
'cuda

(SMALL CAR)
cracker box
roller skate

(SPORTS CAR)
super skate

(VOLKSWAGEN)
Nazi go-cart (SE)
pregnant roller skate (W)

CAR TROUBLE
> hammer jammer (SE)
>
> (UNLOCKED OR OPEN REAR DOOR)
> busted zipper
> gapin' skirt

CARGO (see also TRUCK; WORK)
> load
>
> (DANGEROUS CARGO)
> suicide cargo
>
> (EMPTY LOAD)
> load of sailboat wind
> post holes
>
> (LIGHTWEIGHT SHIPMENT)
> balloon freight
> minnie
> zephyr haul
>
> (LOOSE CARGO)
> kangaroo(ing)
>
> (MEAT SHIPMENT)
> swinging beef
>
> (1,000 POUND SHIPMENT)
> bushel
>
> (OVERLOAD)
> chicken choker
> fat load
>
> (PICK-UP)
> 10-31 (Abbreviated 10-Code)
>
> (RUSH SHIPMENT)
> hot load
>
> (SHIPMENT OF PIGS)
> go-go girls

CARPENTER
  wood butcher (W)
  woodpecker (SE)

CASPAR, WYOMING
  Ghost Town

CATTLE
  Polack kids (SE)

CEMETERY
  boneyard

CHANNEL
  pipeline

  (CHANNEL CBer USUALLY FREQUENTS)
  home channel

  (CHANNEL 1)
  basement (NW)

  (CHANNEL 5)
  nickel channel

  (CHANNEL 10)
  dime channel

  (CHANNEL 15)
  diesel digit

  (CONTACT CHANNEL)
  slaughter house (NW)

  (EMERGENCY CHANNEL)
  Channel 9
  E.R.S. (Emergency Radio Service)

  (OVERCROWDED CHANNEL)
  bad scene

  (TRUCKERS' CHANNEL)
  Channel 10 (MW, W)
  Channel 19

CHANNEL USE

    (ALL CHANNELS ARE BUSY)
    everybody must be walking the dog (SE)

    (CHANNEL 1 WITH SIDEBANDERS TALKING
    ON IT)
    terrible situation (MW)

    (FREE CHANNEL)
    cleaner channel

    (LEAVING THE CHANNEL)
    bug out
    cut out (NW)

    (SCANNING CHANNELS)
    quick trip around the horn

    (SWITCH CHANNELS)
    make a trip
    19-27 ('Official' 10-Code)

    (SWITCH TO HIGHER CHANNEL)
    jump up

    (SWITCH TO LOWER CHANNEL)
    jump down

    (WILL YOU MOVE TO A DIFFERENT
    CHANNEL?)
    QSY
    10-41 ('Official' 10-Code)

CHARLESTON, SOUTH CAROLINA
    Charlie

CHATTANOOGA, TENNESSEE
    Choo-Choo Town (SE)
    Rock City

CHEYENNE, WYOMING
    Rodeo Town

CHICAGO, ILLINOIS
  Big C
  Cattle Town
  Chi Town
  Shy Town
  Wind City
  Windy City

CHILDREN
  anklebiters (NE)
  carpet crawlers (SW)
  crumb crushers (SE)
  drape ape (SW)
  forty-fours (SW)
  muskrats (SE, SW)
  rug rats (W)
  tricycle motors (SW)

CIGARETTES
  cookies

CINCINNATI, OHIO
  Cincy
  Queen City (MW)
  Sin City (MW)

CITY (see also TOWN)
  patch

CLEVELAND, OHIO
  Dirty City
  Iron Town
  Mistake on the Lake
  Smokey City West

CLOSE REAR DOORS OF TRACTOR TRAILER
  close the gates

COAXIAL CABLE (see CB RADIO AND EQUIPMENT)

CODE NAME (see also IDENTIFICATION)
    handle

CODES (see pages 239-244)
    Q-Code
    10-Code (Abbreviated and 'Official')

COFFEE
    black water (SE)
    cup of mud
    hot stuff (SE)
    java
    mud
    road tar
    tar
    thirty weight (SW)

    (DAY-OLD COFFEE)
    Western-style coffee

    (STRONG COFFEE)
    benny chaser
    hundred mile coffee

CONROE, TEXAS
    Miracle City (SW)

CONTACT (see also CB CONVERSATION)

    (MAKE CONTACT)
    raise
    10-19 (Abbreviated 10-Code)

    (NO CONTACT)
    double seven
    negative contact
    negative copy
    pair of sevens
    10-77 ('Official' 10-Code)

CONVOY (see LINE OF VEHICLES USING CB)

CORN — SHELLED
   Texas strawberries (SW)

CORPUS CHRISTI, TEXAS
   Taco Town

CORRECT (see YES)

CRYSTAL (see CB RADIO AND EQUIPMENT)

DALLAS, TEXAS
   Big D (SW)
   Big D City (or Town)

DANGER — CAUTION
   10-30 (Abbreviated 10-Code)

DAUGHTER
   X-Y-D

DAVENPORT, IOWA
   Quad Cities

DAY — WONDERFUL
   pepsi day

DEAD
   gone 10-7 permanently

   (DROP DEAD)
   10-400 (NE)

DENVER, COLORADO
   Big D
   Mile High City (or Town)

DEPARTMENT OF COMMUNICATIONS (Canada)
   D.O.C.

DEPARTMENT OF TRANSPORTATION REPRE-
SENTATIVE
   D.O.T. man
   Fed

DES MOINES, IOWA
  Big D

DETOUR
  busted sidewalk (MW)

DETROIT, MICHIGAN
  Motor City

DIRECTION (see also ROAD — ROAD BEHIND;
  TRIP)
    being *east* (or *north, south, west*)
    *east*bound, struttin' style
    *east*bound, trailer truckin' style
    legalizing *east* (or *north, south, west*)

    (CHANGE DIRECTION; MAKE A U-TURN)
    bang a U-ey (NE)
    flip
    flip-flop
    flipper

    (GOING AWAY FROM HOME)
    going thataway

    (HOMEWARD BOUND)
    dead head
    going thisaway

    (OPPOSITE DIRECTION)
    left shoulder
    we'll be doin' it the other way

    (TURN AROUND)
    flop it (SE)

DIRECTIONAL ANTENNA (see CB RADIO AND
  EQUIPMENT)

DISNEY WORLD, FLORIDA
  Mickey Mouse Town (SE)

DISNEYLAND, CALIFORNIA
  Cinderella World (W)
  Land of Disney (W)

DISTRESS SIGNAL (see EMERGENCY; HELP)

DOCTOR
  man in white (NW)

DOPE PUSHER
  ten-two thousand (10-2000) (W)

DRINK
  suck it up

  (DRINKING PARTY)
  picnic

DRIVE, DRIVING (see also DIRECTION; SPEED; TRIP)
  being *east* (or *north, south, west*)
  cooking
  *east*bound, struttin' style
  knocking
  legalizing *east* (or *north, south, west)*
  mobiling (W)
  motor on
  motoring on (SE)
  move
  on the move
  pedal
  ramble on
  rolling
  shaking it (SE)
  stepping (SE)
  streak
  strut
  struttin'

DRIVE, DRIVING *(continued)*
    trailer truck it
    truck forward
    truck on
    walkin'
    wheeling around

(BACKING UP A SEMI AROUND A SHARP CURVE)
jacking it around

(BRAKE; BRAKE QUICKLY)
anchor it
lay on the air
put on the air
set it down

(COAST)
pedal
pedal along and wait on you (SE)

(DRIVE AND SLEEP, ALTERNATELY)
roll and rest

(DRIVE VEHICLE FORWARD AND BACK TO GET OUT OF MUD OR SNOW)
rock it

(DRIVING A TRUCK)
*east*bound, trailer truckin' style
pushing a rig
trailer trucking 18

(DRIVING EMPTY ON GAS)
dead heading
sailboat fuel

(DRIVING IN THE MIDDLE LANE) (see also ROAD)
pedaling in the middle (SE)

(DRIVING ON BACK ROADS AT NIGHT TO AVOID WEIGH STATIONS)
boondock
working for the moonlight express

(DRIVING ON ROAD SHOULDER)
dusting

(DRIVING UNSAFELY) (see also DRIVER; SPEED)
smoking with the devil

(DRIVING WITHOUT A LOAD; DRIVING AN EMPTY TRUCK)
dead heading
hauling post holes
loaded with sailboat fuel
loaded with Volkswagen radiators
sailboat fuel

(FOLLOWING CLOSELY BEHIND ANOTHER VEHICLE)
bird doggin'
bumper jumper
'gating
holding onto your mud flaps (MW)
livin' dead
tailgating

(GETTING OFF THE EXPRESSWAY)
peeling off (SE)

(GOING OVER THE MOUNTAIN)
crossing the hump

(JACKKNIFE)
double-up

(KEEP MOVING)
get trucking
keep on trucking

(LEAVING OR ENTERING A TOLL ROAD)
getting off (or on) the green stamp

(LOSE TRACTION)
spin out

(MAKING THE BEST POSSIBLE TIME)
he's layin', he's stayin'

(MOVE YOUR VEHICLE UP; COME THIS WAY)
bring it on
bring it up
bring on your machine
bring yourself on in (or up) (SE)
brought it on
brought yourself on in (or up)

(PASS ANOTHER VEHICLE)
blow the doors off
blowing your doors in
do you hear someone knocking on your back
   door?
shove 'er down and come around (SW)
smoke him

(PASSED BY ANOTHER VEHICLE)
blew my doors off
dusted my britches (SE, SW)

(RAN OFF THE SIDE OF THE ROAD)
dropped it off the shoulder (SE)

(SKID)
hydroplane

(SLOWED OR STOPPED BY OBSTRUCTION)
tied up

(STOP DRIVING)
turn over

(STRADDLING TWO LANES)
pedaling in the middle

DRIVE SAFELY (see also SIGN-OFF)
>   good truckin'
>   have a safe one and a fine one
>   have a safe one and a sound one (SE)
>   keep 'em between the ditches (SE)
>   keep the rolling side down and the shiny side up (SE)
>   keep the rubber side down
>   keep the shiny side up and the dirty side down (NW)
>   keep the shiny side up and the greasy side down (NW)
>   keep the shiny side up and the rolling side down
>   keep the wheels spinning (SE)
>   keep your nose between the ditches and smokey out of your britches
>   keep your wheels spinning and the beavers grinning
>   safe truckin'
>   stay between the jumps and bumps
>   stay between the jumps and the bumps and truck over all the humps
>   truck 'em easy
>   truck 'em light (SE)
>   two miles of ditches for every mile of road, keep your rig in the middle (MW)
>   watch the pavement (SE)

DRIVER
>   concentrator

>   (DRIVER MOVING TOO SLOWLY)
>   dead foot
>   feather foot (SE)
>   heavy foot
>   lead foot

>   (DRIVER OF SPORTS CAR)
>   skate jockey

(DRIVER WHO BRAKES TOO FREQUENTLY)
fake brake
peg leg

(DRIVER WHO HOGS ROAD)
eight-miler
hoo-hooner
road hog

(DRIVER WHO IS CAUGHT SPEEDING) (see
also SPEEDING; VEHICLE)
pigeon

(DRIVER WHO IS LOST OR CONFUSED)
Alice in Wonderland

(DRIVER WHO IS OVER-CAUTIOUS)
Mr. Clean

(DRIVER WHO IS OVER-CONFIDENT)
tailboard artist

(DRIVER WHO IS RECKLESS, OR INEPT)
cowboy
grandstand jockey
harvey wallbanger (MW)
rude dude
sheep herder
tiger in the tank (MW)

(DRIVER WHO IS SPEEDING) (see also
DRIVING; SPEED)
aviator
roger ramjet (MW)
roger roller skate (W)

(DRUNK DRIVER)
willy weaver

(MOTORCYCLIST)
Evel Knievel

(TAXICAB DRIVER)
cabbie

(TRUCK DRIVER)
big dummy
buddy (SE)
chicken choker
cottonpicker
gear jammer
guy (MW, NE)
hard ankle
professional
road jockey
truck jockey
truck stop commando
truckin' guy (NE, MW)
working man (MW)

(TRUCKER ATTRACTIVE TO WOMEN)
beaver cleaver

(TRUCKER DRIVING A DUMP TRUCK)
dump chump

(TRUCKER HAULING EXPLOSIVES)
suicide jockey

(TRUCKER HAULING LIVE ANIMALS)
goat 'n shoat man
shoat and goat conductor

(TRUCKER — INDEPENDENT)
gypsy

(TRUCKER — INEXPERIENCED)
boll weevil

(TRUCKER WITH FANCY TRUCK)
cowboy trucker

(TRUCKER WITH LOW SENIORITY)
woodchuck

(TRUCKER WITHOUT A STEADY JOB)
floater

(TRUCKERS — TOUGH GROUP OF)
  B-A-R Team
  mafia squad

DRIVING PARTNER
  other half
  ride shot gun
  running shot gun
  shot gun
  swamper

DULUTH, MINNESOTA
  The Little Twin
  Twin Forts

EARS
  flappers (NW)

EAST COAST
  The Dirty Side

EAT (see also RESTAURANT; STOPS)
  chowdown
  put on the feedbag

EDISON BRIDGE (Perth Amboy, New Jersey)
  Top of the World (NE)

EL PASO, TEXAS
  Border Town
  Burrito City
  Sun City
  Taco City (or Town)

ELECTRICIAN
  sparkie (W)

ELECTRONIC INDUSTRIES ASSOCIATION
  EIA

EMERGENCY
    niner
    10-33 ('Official' and Abbreviated 10-Codes)
    10-34 ('Official' 10-Code)
    thirty-three

EMPLOYER (see also WORK)
    Where do you get your green stamps?
    Who do you pull for?

EMPLOYMENT LOCATION
    junkyard
    salt mines
    work twenty

ENGINE — BIG
    full of vitamins (SE)
    great big sprocket (SE)

    (TRUCK ENGINE)
    iron lunger
    jimmie

    (TWO-CYCLE ENGINE)
    bumble bee

ENGINE COVER
    dog house (NW)

ERIE, PENNSYLVANIA
    Big E
    Dead City

EUPHEMISM FOR OBSCENE OR PROFANE
  REMARK
    duck plucker
    flakey
    mercy
    mercy sakes
    mercy snakes

EXHAUST PIPE
    stack

EXPRESSWAY (see ROAD)

**FCC; FCC REPRESENTATIVE (see also DEPART-
MENT OF COMMUNICATIONS)**
    Big Daddy
    candy man
    Charley
    Cousin Charley
    Daddy-O (NW)
    Fed
    fox Charley
    fox hunter
    Friendly Candy Company (NE)
    Friendly Cousin Charley
    Funny Candy Company
    Gestapo
    panic in the streets
    10-1000 (W)
    The Man
    Uncle Charley

FCC RULES
    Part 15
    Part 95
    prescription
    quiet hours

    (FCC RULES VIOLATION)
    10-30 ('Official' 10-Code)

    (FCC RULES VIOLATOR) (see also CB OPER-
ATOR; CB USE)
    scofflaw

FARGO, NORTH DAKOTA
    Fargo Land

FARGO, NORTH DAKOTA *(continued)*
Little Twins
Windy City

FIFTY-FIVE MILES PER HOUR (see SPEED)

FIGHT
knuckle buster (W)

FIRE; SMOKE
hot pants

FIRE — LOCATION OF
10-70 ('Official' 10-Code)

FIRE STATION
snake den (SW)

FIREMAN
man in a slicker (NW)

FLASHING LIGHTS (see also LAW ENFORCE-MENT VEHICLES)
bubble machine
bubblegum machine
colors going up
gumball machine
red wheel (MW)

FLATTERY
act of mental gratification (NE)
stroking

FLORIDA
Bikini State

FOG (see WEATHER CONDITIONS)

FOOD
biscuits and gravy

FORREST CITY, ARKANSAS
Bar City (SE)

FORT LAUDERDALE, FLORIDA
Beach City

FORT WORTH, TEXAS
Cow Town
Twin City

FOUL-UP
fubar
snafu

FREQUENCY
A-F
freq (MW)
R-F

(CB FREQUENCIES)
Class A Station (460-470 MHz)
Class C Station (26.96-27.26, 72-76 MHz)
Class D Station (26.96-27.26 MHz)
Eleven-Meter Band (27 MHz)

(CHECK MY FREQUENCY ON CHANNEL)
10-93 ('Official' 10-Code)

(POLICE RADAR FREQUENCY)
X-band

(WHAT IS MY EXACT FREQUENCY?)
QRG

FRIEND
ace
big dummy
buddy (SE)
cottonpicker
good buddy
guy (MW, NE)

FUEL (see GAS)

GAMBLE (LOSE MONEY AT THE HORSE RACES)
    feed the ponies (or horses) (SW)

    (GAMBLERS)
    rolling dominos (MW)

GARAGE
    barn
    hangar

GARAGE SUPERINTENDENT
    chief hood lifter

GARY, INDIANA
    Yellow Air
    Yellow Breath

GAS; FUEL
    giggle juice (SW)
    go juice
    go-go juice
    juice
    motion-lotion (SE)
    motion-potion
    petro
    push water (SW)
    pusholine (SW)
    V-8 juice

    (BAD FUEL)
    slop

    (LOW OR EMPTY ON GAS)
    sailboat fuel

GAS TANK
    juice jug (MW)
    lotion bottle

GEARS

> (HIGH GEAR)
> going-home hole
> pay hole
>
> (LOWEST GEAR, OR GEARS)
> creeper gear
> grandma
> granny gear
>
> (PERSON WHO GRINDS GEARS)
> gear bonger
> gear jammer
>
> (SHIFT INTO LOWER GEAR)
> grab one
> kick down
>
> (SHIFT TOO SLOWLY)
> drag down
>
> (TAKE OUT OF GEAR)
> Georgia overdrive
> Mexican overdrive
> midnight overdrive

GEORGIA
> Peach State

GIRL (see WOMAN)

GLOVE COMPARTMENT
> hip pocket

GOD BLESS YOU
> G-B-Y

GOOD-BYE (see SIGN-OFF)

GRAND RAPIDS, MICHIGAN
> Chair City

GREAT FALLS, MONTANA
High Water

GREEN BAY, WISCONSIN
Title Town

HAM RADIO OPERATOR
ham

(GATHERING OF HAM RADIO OPERATORS)
hamboree
hamfest

HARTFORD, CONNECTICUT
Stag City

HATE AND DISSENT
H & D

HEADLIGHTS
eyeballs

(BLINK HEADLIGHTS)
shake the lights

HEAR (see METER; RECEPTION; UNDERSTAND)

HEAVEN
big skip lane

HEIGHT OF TRUCK
How tall are you? (MW)

HELICOPTER (see also LAW ENFORCEMENT VEHICLES)
chopper

HELLO (see CB CONVERSATION)

HELP (see also EMERGENCY)

(AMBULANCE NEEDED)
10-38 ('Official' 10-Code)

(ASSIST MOTORIST)
10-46 ('Official' 10-Code)

(POLICE NEEDED)
10-200 ('Official' 10-Code)

(WRECKER NEEDED)
10-37 ('Official' 10-Code)

HITCHHIKER (TEENAGED)
truckin' teenager

HOLLYWOOD, CALIFORNIA
Tinsel City (or Town) (W)

HOME
casa (SW)

(HOME LOCATION)
home port (SE)
home 10-20
home twenty
10-85 ('Official' 10-Code)

HOMOSEXUAL
lollipop (MW)
10-1000 (NE)

(MALE HOMOSEXUAL)
sissy squad (NE)
three-legged beaver

HOPKINSVILLE, KENTUCKY
H Town (MW, SE, SW)

HOT SPRINGS, ARKANSAS
Hot Water City

HOTEL OR MOTEL (see also STOPS)
flop box
nap trap

(RESERVE HOTEL ROOM FOR _____)
10-81 ('Official' 10-Code)

HOUSTON, TEXAS
Astro Town
Astrodome City (SE)
Dome City
Space City

HOW ARE YOU?
How you be?
Howzit?

HUNTING SEASON
Daniel Boone time

HUNTSVILLE, ALABAMA
Rocket City
Space City

HUSBAND (see also SPOUSE)
better half
buffalo
M-O-M (SW)
O-M
old man
other half
X-Y-L (MW)
X-Y-M

(EX-HUSBAND)
X

IDENTIFICATION
callsign
I.D.

(CODE NAME OF CBer)
handle

(QSL CARD)
wallpaper (NW)

(REQUEST FOR IDENTIFICATION)
QRA
10-28 ('Official' 10-Code)
Who is in the four-wheeler?
Who is on the mike?
Who we got on that end?
Who we got there?
Who's in that 18-wheeler?

(WHAT ARE YOU DRIVING?)
What are you pushing?

(WHAT IS YOUR CODE NAME?)
What's your handle?

(WHAT KIND OF TRUCK ARE YOU DRIVING?)
What's your eighteen?

ILLINOIS
Lincoln Country

ILLINOIS SECRETARY OF STATE OFFICE
S-O-S

INDIANA
Hoosier State

INDIANAPOLIS, INDIANA
Circle City (MW)
Speed Town

INFORMATION
poop

(CONFIDENTIAL INFORMATION)
10-35 ('Official' 10-Code)

(LICENSE/PERMIT INFORMATION)
10-27 (Abbreviated 10-Code)

(OWNERSHIP INFORMATION)
10-28 (Abbreviated 10-Code)

(RECORDS CHECK)
10-29 (Abbreviated 10-Code)

INSECTS ON THE WINDSHIELD
bugs on the glass

INTERFERENCE (see RECEPTION; SIGNAL;
TRANSMIT)

IRVINE, CALIFORNIA
Buggerhole Bunch (W)

JACKSON, MISSISSIPPI
Capital J (SE)

JACKSON, TENNESSEE
J Town (SE)

JAIL
pokey
slammer (W)

JAMBOREE (see CB GATHERING)

KALAMAZOO, MICHIGAN
Guitar City

KANSAS
Cattle State

KANSAS CITY, KANSAS
K.C. Town

KANSAS CITY, MISSOURI
Beef City
K.C. Town

KARATE EXPERT
jumpin' bean (SE)

KENTUCKY
Blue Grass State
Whiskey State

KISSES (see also LOVE AND KISSES)
forty-fours
squeeze-n-eights (NE)
truckloads of 88's (NE)

KNOXVILLE, TENNESSEE
K Town (SE)

LAKE CHARLES, LOUISIANA
Charlie Town (SW)

LANE

(EMPTY LEFT LANE)
wide side

(MIDDLE LANE)
Wallace lane

(PASSING LANE)
bullet lane (SE)
bumper lane
fifty dollar lane (SE)
green stamp lane (SE)
left lane
mama's lane
milford lane
monfort lane (SW, W. MW)
monster lane (MW)
show-off lane (SE)
side door (SE)

(RIGHT HAND OR SLOW LANE)
McLean lane

LAS VEGAS, NEVADA
Dice City
Divorce City (W)
Gambling Town
Lost Wages
Sin City (W)

LAW ENFORCEMENT (see also FCC; LAW EN-
FORCEMENT VEHICLE; LAW ENFORCEMENT
WITH CB; POLICE ACTIVITIES; RADAR)
> bear
> bearded buddy (SE)
> big brother
> black and white
> blue and white (MW)
> bull
> Jack Rabbit (W)
> John Law
> long arm
> man in blue (NW)
> mouse ears
> Peter Rabbit (W)
> pig
> politz-eye
> porky bear (SE)
> rover
> salt and pepper (MW)
> shamus
> smoke
> smoke 'em up bear (SE)
> smoker
> smokey
> teddy bear
> The Man
> white rabbit
>
> (FEDERAL GOVERNMENT OFFICIALS)
> President's men (MW)
>
> (LOCAL POLICE)
> blue boy (SE, SW)
> city kitty (MW)
> country joe (MW)
> little bear (SE)
> local bear

(LOCAL POLICE—*continued*)

local boy (SE)
local constabulary
local smokel (NE)
local smokey
local yokel (SE)
mickey mitchell (SE)

(NATIONAL GUARD)
week-end warriors

(MISSOURI POLICE)
Dudley Do-Right

(MOTORCYCLE POLICE)
Evel Knievel smokey (SW)
Mickey Mouse metro on a tricycle
smokey two-wheeler (W)

(MOUNTED POLICE)
smokey on four legs (NYC and Chicago)

(NEW YORK CITY MUFFLER CONTROL)
noise machine (NE)

(NEW YORK CITY TUNNEL AUTHORITY
POLICE)
hole in the wall rats

(NEW YORK STATE DEPARTMENT OF AIR
POLLUTION)
smoking habit

(PARK POLICE)
grasshopper

(PHILADELPHIA, PENNSYLVANIA POLICE)
Rizzo's Raiders (NE)

(POLICEWOMAN)
girlie bear (SE)
honey bear
lady bear

(POLICEWOMAN—*continued*)

mama bear
mama smokey (SE)
smokey beaver (SE)

(ROOKIE POLICE)
baby bear

(SHERIFF'S DEPARTMENT)
county mounty (SE)
cub scouts (NW)
mounty

(STATE TROOPER)
barnie (SW)
big hat
blue jeans (MW)
boogie man (NW)
boy scout (NE)
Kojak (SE)
pink panther (SE, SW)
polar bear
sloppy joe (SE)
smokey bear (SE)
smokey the bear
state bear
whatevers
white knight

LAW ENFORCEMENT VEHICLE
(HELICOPTER)
air bear
bear in the air
bear in the sky
bird in the air
chopper in the air
eye in the sky
fly in the sky
mounties in the sky

(HELICOPTER—*continued*)
sky bear
sky mounty
smokey chopper
spy in the sky
tattletale

(HORSE-MOUNTED POLICE)
smokey on four legs (NYC and Chicago)

(MOTORCYCLE)
Evel Knievel smokey (SW)
Mickey Mouse metro on a tricycle (SE)
smokey two-wheeler (W)

(POLICE CAR)
black and white
blue light
hound on the ground (NE)
mouse ears
pole cat (SW)
taxi
Tijuana taxi (MW)

(POLICE CAR — DISGUISED)
funny bunny

(POLICE CAR — HIDDEN)
hiding in the bushes, sitting under the leaves
   (SE)
sitting under the leaves
sneaky snake (SE)

(POLICE CAR — NEW YORK STATE)
sunoco (NE)
sunoco mobile (NE)
sunoco special (NE)

(POLICE CAR — ON MEDIAN)
hiding in the grass (SE)
smokey grazing grass

(POLICE CAR — STOPPED)
diamond in the rough (SW)
smokey dozing

(POLICE CAR — UNMANNED)
decoy
dummy
dummy car
scarecrow

(POLICE CAR — UNMARKED)
brown paper bag (NE)
envelope
pink panther (SE)
plain brown (*or other color*) wrapper
wrapper

(POLICE CAR — WITH CB) (see also LAW
ENFORCEMENT WITH CB)
black and white CBer (W)
pink panther (SE)

(POLICE CAR — WITH RADAR) (see also
RADAR)
camera car

(POLICE CAR — WITH RADAR, CHASE CAR
AHEAD)
one in the shower, one in the bathtub watching
  (NE)

(POLICE RADAR CHASE CAR)
catch car
chase car
chaser
fetch 'em up (NE)
hound dog (SE)

(POLICE VEHICLE WITH FLASHING LIGHTS)
advertising
bubble machine

(POLICE WITH LIGHTS—*continued*)
bubblegum machine
fireworks
freight light
lit candles
party hat
party hat on
party hat on the shelf (SE)
red wheel (MW)
snoopers
Tijuana taxi (MW)

LAW ENFORCEMENT WITH CB
black and white CBer (W)
green CBer
papa bear (MW)
smokey with ears
sneaky snake
white rabbit with ears

LAWNMOWER
oversized grasshopper (MW)

LAWRENCE, KANSAS
River City

LIBERAL, KANSAS
Pancake City

LICENSE PLATES
tags

LICENSE

(CB LICENSE)
glory card (NE)
station license

(DRIVER'S LICENSE)
bouncing cardboard

(LEARNER'S PERMIT)
training wheels

LINE OF VEHICLES USING CB
    convoy
    front door, back door, rocking chair
    shake the trees (or bushes) and rake the leaves

    (DRIVERS STAYING IN CONTACT ON ROAD)
    running together (SE)

    (FIRST CB VEHICLE)
    beat the bushes
    breaking wind (MW)
    clearing the way
    front door
    front end (MW)
    front yard
    rubber duck
    shake the bushes (NW)
    shake the leaves
    shake the trees

    (MIDDLE CB VEHICLE)
    easy chair (NW)
    rocking chair
    sitting in the saddle (SE)

    (LAST CB VEHICLE)
    back door
    back door closed
    back door sealed up
    back door shut
    hind end (SE, SW)
    rake the leaves
    sweep the leaves
    watch your donkey
    wipe the bugs off your plates

(PUT REAR CB VEHICLE OUT OF RANGE)
run out the front end (SE)

LINEAR AMPLIFIER (see CB RADIO AND EQUIPMENT)

LIQUOR
    cactus juice (SW)
    corn squeezings (NE)
    corn syrup (NE)
    joy juice
    juice
    Kool Aid
    ninety weight (SW)
    red-eye
    spring water (SW)

LIQUOR STORE
    corn cellar

LISTEN TO THE CB (MONITOR) (see also RECEPTION; SIGN-OFF — THROUGH TRANSMITTING BUT MONITORING; UNDERSTAND)
    copying the mail
    monitor
    on standby
    on the by
    on the side
    reading the mail
    sittin' by
    stand by
    10-10
    ten-ten and listnin' in

    (ARE YOU LISTENING?)
    Got your ears on?

    (DO YOU HEAR ME?)
    Do you copy?

(DO YOU HEAR ME?—*continued*)
Do you have a copy?
Got a copy?
Xerox? (SE)
You gotta copy on me?

(HEAR)
read

(LISTEN HABITUALLY TO A PARTICULAR CHANNEL)
hang out

(LISTEN TO CHANNEL #)
basketball on Channel (#)
monitor

(MUST CONTINUE TO LISTEN)
hung up

(PERSON IS NOT LISTENING)
peanut butter in his ears (SW)

LITTER
garbage (MW)

LITTERBUG
garbageman (MW)

LITTLE ROCK, ARKANSAS
Rock City (SE, SW)

LOCATION
10-20 (Abbreviated and 'Official' 10-Codes)
twenty

(ARE YOU RETURNING TO (*location*)?)
QRF

(ARRIVED AT SCENE)
10-23 (Abbreviated 10-Code)

(HOW FAR AWAY ARE YOU?)
QRB

(IN THE MEDIAN)
in the grass (SE)

(LOCATION OF EXIT OR TURN)
turn twenty

(REQUEST FOR LOCATION)
What's your twenty?

(SPEED TRAP LOCATED AT _____)
10-73 (Official' 10-Code)

(WHERE ARE YOU GOING, WHERE DID YOU
COME FROM?)
QRD

LONG DISTANCE
D-X

LONG ISLAND (NEW YORK)
Shark Town

LONGMONT, COLORADO
Laughin' City

LOOK; LOOK AT; SEE
eyeball
got my eyeballs peeled
lay an eye on it
put an eyeball on him (SE, SW)
shot an eyeball on it (MW)

(LOOK AT ANOTHER VEHICLE WHILE
DRIVING)
mobile eyeball

(LOOK AT, OR FOR, WOMEN)
beaver hunt
beaver patrol
check the seat covers

(LOOK AT WOMEN—*continued*)
rubberneck
window shopping (NE)

(LOOK AT PASSENGERS)
check the seat covers

(LOOK AWAY FROM THE ROAD AT TREES)
buying an orchard

(LOOK FOR POLICE COMING FROM
BEHIND)
watch your donkey

(SLOW DOWN TO LOOK AT ACCIDENT OR
BREAK-DOWN)
rubberneck

LOOKERS
rubberneckers

LOS ANGELES, CALIFORNIA
Angel City
Shakey City

LOUISVILLE, KENTUCKY
Derby City (or Town) (MW)

LOVE AND KISSES (see also BEST WISHES;
KISSES; SIGN-OFF)
double eighty-eights
eighty-eights

MACON, GEORGIA
Macon Town

MAINE
Pine Tree State (NE)

MAKING LOVE
making motors for tricycles
six-ten (NE)

MAN (see also HUSBAND; SPOUSE; PERSON)
    buffalo
    hard ankle
    jock
    X-Y-N (SW)

    (LONG-HAIRED MALE)
    beaver with a kick stand (SW)

    (MALE HOMOSEXUALS)
    sissy squad (NE)
    10-1000 (NE)
    three-legged beavers

    (MAN WITH LITTLE PERSONALITY OR
    COURAGE)
    whimp (NW)

    (OLD MAN) (see also HUSBAND; SPOUSE)
    O-M

MARIJUANA
    grass
    whackey tobackey (SW)

MARINE BASE
    green machine

MARINE UNIFORM
    pickle suit (W)

MARKEL INSURANCE COMPANY REPRESENTA-
    TIVE
    Mark-L man
    Markel man

MASTURBATE
    chicken choker
    choke the chicken
    if you can't use it, abuse it (MW)
    lope your mule (SW)

MASTURBATE (*continued*)
    stroke your lizard (SW)
    three-five

MEAL (see EAT; RESTAURANT; STOPS)

MECHANIC
    hood lifter
    maniac
    mik-e-nik (SW)

    (BAD MECHANIC)
    Attilla the Hun
    Ghengis Khan

MEDIAN
    grass

MEET
    eyeball
    eyeball it (SE)
    eyeball to eyeball (SE, SW)
    rub eyeballs

    (REPORT IN PERSON)
    10-22 ('Official' 10-Code)

    (REPORT TO MEET)
    10-25 (Abbreviated 10-Code)

    (SEE YOU IN PERSON)
    put an eye on 'ya

MEETING PLACE (see also LOCATION)
    meeting twenty
    M20 (SE)

MEMPHIS, TENNESSEE
    Big M (SE)
    River City (SE)

MESSAGE (see also CB CONVERSATION)
    copy
    10-14 (Abbreviated 10-Code)

    (DISREGARD MESSAGE)
    breeze it
    10-22 (Abbreviated 10-Code)
    10-26 ('Official' 10-Code)

    (HAVE YOU ANYTHING FOR ME?)
    QRU

    (HOW MANY MESSAGES DO YOU HAVE FOR
    ME?)
    QTC

    (MESSAGE DELIVERED)
    10-15 (Abbreviated 10-Code)
    10-39 ('Official' 10-Code)

    (MESSAGE FOR YOU)
    10-44 ('Official' 10-Code)

    (MESSAGE RECEIVED)
    four
    four D
    four roger
    four ten
    got the copy
    roger
    roger-D
    10-4 ('Official' 10-Code)
    10-69 ('Official' 10-Code)
    ten-forty
    ten roger
    that's a copy

    (RELAY MESSAGE)
    10-5 (Abbreviated and 'Official' 10-Codes)

(REPEAT MESSAGE)
come again
come on back
say again
say what?
10-9 (Abbreviated and 'Official' 10-Codes)

(REPLY TO MESSAGE)
10-16 (Abbreviated 10-Code)

(SHALL I REPEAT MESSAGE?)
QSM

METER
pound meter
S meter
S/rf meter

(I WILL GIVE YOU A RADIO CHECK)
10-32 ('Official' 10-Code)

(METER READING)
pounds
radio check
voice check

(REQUEST FOR METER READING)
How do you read me?
What am I putting on you?
What kind of copy?

METS BASEBALL FAN
loser (NE)

MIAMI, FLORIDA
Big M

MILEPOST
green lollipop (SW)
lollipop
marker

MILEPOST *(continued)*
    milemarker
    post

MILK
    cow squeezings (NE)
    vitamin A (NE)

MILWAUKEE, WISCONSIN
    Beer City (MW)

MINNEAPOLIS, MINNESOTA
    Big Twin
    Twin City

MINNEAPOLIS/ST. PAUL, MINNESOTA
    Twin Cities

MINUTES
    ticks (NE)

MIRROR
    screen

MISSISSIPPI
    Magnolia State (SE)

MOLINE, ILLINOIS
    Quad City

MONEY
    bread
    green stamps
    greens
    lettuce (W)
    S and H green stamps
    trading stamps

MONITOR (see LISTEN)

MONTANA
    Monty

MONTGOMERY, ALABAMA
   Monkey Town (SE)

MORSE CODE
   C-W

MOTEL (see HOTEL)

MOTORCYCLE (see also LAW ENFORCEMENT
   VEHICLES)
   two-wheeler

MOUNTAIN
   hump

MOUTH
   soup cooler

MOVIE
   flick

   (DRIVE-IN MOVIE)
   outdoor TV (W)

MOVING (see DRIVING; SPEED)

NAME (see IDENTIFICATION)

NASHVILLE, TENNESSEE
   Guitar Town (SE, MW)
   Music City (SE)
   Musical City (SE)
   Nastyville (SE)
   Opryland

NEDERLAND, TEXAS
   Windmill City (SW)

NEIGHBORS WHO GET TV INTERFERENCE
   FROM CB TRANSMISSIONS
   indians
   riot squad

NERVOUS ABOUT SPEAKING ON CB
    mike fright

NETWORK

    (NETWORK CLEAR)
    10-64 ('Official' 10-Code)

    (NETWORK DIRECTED TO _____)
    10-63 ('Official' 10-Code)

NEW JERSEY
    Brown Cow
    Dirty Side

NEW ORLEANS, LOUISIANA
    Dixie Town
    Fun City
    Jazz City
    Mardi Gras Town
    Superdome City (SE)

NEW YORK, NEW YORK
    Chapter 13
    Fun City (NE)
    Naked City
    The Big Apple (NE)
    The Big Lady
    The Dirty Side

NEWPORT, KENTUCKY
    Sin City (MW)

NIAGARA FALLS, NEW YORK
    Water Barrel

NIGHT
    dark time (NW)

NIGHTCLUBBING
    boogieing

NO (see also CONTACT — NO CONTACT)
double seven
negatine (SE, SW, W)
negative
negatore
negatory
suppository (SE)
10-10 ('Official' 10-Code)
10-74 ('Official' 10-Code)

NONSENSE
hang it in your ear (W)

NORFOLK, VIRGINIA
Sailor City

NOW
one time

NURSES
panhandlers (MW)

OAKLAND, CALIFORNIA
Big Oak

OBSCENE GESTURE
finger wave (SE)
pitch a parakeet (SE)

OFF (TURN OFF THE CB RADIO)
cut the co-ax
down and gone (SE, MW)
going down
pull switches
pull the big one (NW)
pull the big switch
pulling the plug

OHIO
Buckeye State

OKAY?
How about it?

OKLAHOMA CITY, OKLAHOMA
Oil City
Okie

PADUCAH, KENTUCKY
River City (MW)

PALESTINE, TEXAS
Holy City (SW)

PARADE
wagon train (MW)

PARK THE TRAILER
spot the body

PARKED (see STOPPED)

PARKING LOT — UNPAVED
dirt floor

PASS ANOTHER VEHICLE (see DRIVING)

PASSENGER (see also DRIVER; DRIVING PARTNER)
seat cover

(ANIMAL IN VEHICLE)
jaws (MW)

(ATTRACTIVE FEMALE PASSENGER)
fancy seat cover

(PASSENGER IN TRUCK)
shot gun

PASSENGER SIDE OF VEHICLE
blind side

PEDESTRIAN ON THE ROAD
boot jockey

PEP PILLS
  cockleburrs (SE)
  mollies
  Virginia vitamins (SW)
  west coast turnarounds (NE, SW)

  (TRAVELING ON PEP PILLS)
  going with the grain

PERMANENT TRANSCEIVER (see CB RADIO AND
  EQUIPMENT)

PERSON (see also CB OPERATOR; FRIEND; MAN;
  WOMAN)
  flake (MW)
  snuff skeeter

  (DUMB PERSON)
  ding-a-ling
  lid
  turkey (W)

  (FAT PERSON)
  panty stretcher

  (GOOD-LOOKING PERSON)
  finger-licking good

  (I — FIRST PERSON SINGULAR)
  we

  (IMPORTANT PERSON; EXECUTIVE OR
  OFFICIAL)
  brass
  fish
  muckety-muck
  mucky-muck

  (NAIVE PERSON)
  Bambi

(NAIVE PERSON—*continued*)
Easter Bunny

(PEOPLE PRESENT)
twelves

(PERSON ACTING RUDE, NUTS, OR MEAN)
flakey

(PERSON — INSULTING TERM [euphemism])
musqueeter
pea picker (NE)

(TEENAGER)
bubblegummer

(VISITORS PRESENT)
10-12 ('Official' 10-Code)

PHILADELPHIA, PENNSYLVANIA
Bicentennial City
Big Brother
Flag Town (NE)
Liberty City
Philly
Philly Town

PHOENIX, ARIZONA
Cactus Patch
Sun City

PIGS
four-legged go-go dancers (SE)

PILOT
air jockey

PITTSBURGH, PENNSYLVANIA
Pot Hole Town
Smokey City

PITTSBURGH, PENNSYLVANIA *(continued)*
    Steel City
    Superbowl City

POLICE ACTIVITIES (see also HELP; LAW EN-
    FORCEMENT; LAW ENFORCEMENT VEHICLE;
    LAW ENFORCEMENT WITH CB; RADAR)

    (POLICE EVERYWHERE)
    bears are crawling (SE)
    bears wall-to-wall
    dirty with bears
    flip-flopping bears
    nightcrawlers (SE)
    nobody knows where the teddy bear goes (SE)
    open season (SE)
    smoke signals
    smokey's thick (NE)
    someone spilled honey on the road (NW)
    wall-to-wall bears
    Yellowstone Park
    you're not the only one on the road

    (POLICE FOLLOWING)
    foot in the carburetor

    (POLICE GIVING OUT SPEEDING TICKETS)
    bagging them (NE)
    grab bagging
    green stamp collector
    monkeys looking for bananas at *(location)*
    paper hanger (SE, SW, W)
    pigeon plucker
    plucking chickens
    pulling 'em down
    sandbagging

    (POLICE IN HELICOPTER)
    air bear

(POLICE IN HELICOPTER—*continued*)
bear in the air
bear in the sky
bird in the air (SE)
chopper in the air
eye in the sky
fly in the sky
mounty in the sky (SE)
sky bear
sky mounty
smokey chopper
spy in the sky (SE)
tattletale

(POLICE LOCATION REPORT)
bear report
bear situation
bear story (SE)
fix
left shoulder
smoke (smokey) report

(POLICE NOT AROUND) (see also ROAD
CLEAR OF POLICE AND OBSTRUCTIONS)
all clean

(POLICE ON THE MOVE)
bears are crawling
flip-flopping bears
rolling bears (SE)
running bear
smokey on the move
smokey on rubber

(POLICE OUT OF PATROL CAR)
smokey on the ground

(POLICE USING EXCESS AUTHORITY)
bear hug
pig

POLICE STATION
> bear cage
> bear cave (W)
> bears' den
> bears' lair
> zoo

PORNOGRAPHY
> comic books
> funny books

PORT

> (HAVE YOU LEFT PORT?)
> QTO

> (WILL YOU ENTER PORT?)
> QTP

PORT ARTHUR, TEXAS
> P.A. Town (SW)
> Prince Albert Town (SW)

PORTLAND, OREGON
> Big Port
> The City of Roses

PORTLAND, TENNESSEE
> Strawberry City

POSITIVE (see YES)

POWER (see also RADIO SIGNAL)

> (EFFECTIVE RADIATED POWER)
> E-R-P

> (MAXIMUM POWER)
> five watts
> peak
> peak power

> (PEAK ENVELOPE POWER)
> P-E-P

(POWER RATIO)
D-B
decibel

(PUTTING OUT POWER)
running

(VARYING POWER OUTPUT)
amplitude modulation (A-M)

PRETENDING
stupen (SE)

PROSTITUTE
dress for sale (SW)
free ride (W)
little bit (SE, MW)
pavement princess
snuff-dipper
trick babe (SE)
truck stop annie
truck stop waitress (NE)

(CHEAP PROSTITUTE)
Polack 50¢ piece (NE)

(MASSAGE PARLOR ON WHEELS)
camper (NE)

PROVIDENCE, RHODE ISLAND
Ivy Town

PUEBLO, COLORADO
Steel City

RACE HORSE
four-legged beast (W)

RADAR (POLICE WITH RADAR) (see also LAW
ENFORCEMENT VEHICLE; POLICE)
bear making like Buck Rogers (SW)
bear taking pictures
bear trap

(POLICE WITH RADAR) *(continued)*

bears are crawling (SE)
bears wall-to-wall
brush your teeth and comb your hair (NW)
camera
double barrel
electric teeth (SE)
folding camera
green stamp collector
gun runner (SE)
hemorrhoid with a polaroid (MW, SE)
instamatic
kodak (SE)
kodiak with a kodak
Kojak with a kodak
man with a gun (SE)
movie camera
movies
photographer
picture box
picture taker
pictures
picture-taking machine
polaroid
portrait painter (SE)
shot gun
smile and comb your hair (SE, SW)
smoke screen (SE)
smokey with a camera
sniper
taking pictures
taking pictures each way
two-way radar
wall-to-wall bears (NE)
X-ray machine

(POLICE WITH RADAR) *(continued)*
X-raying
Yellowstone Park (NW, SE)

RADAR DETECTION DEVICE
fuzz buster
seeing eye dog

RADIO SIGNAL (see also POWER; RECEPTION; TRANSMIT)
output
putting out
"S" units
trip

(ARE YOU EXPERIENCING INTERFERENCE?)
QRM

(ARE YOU EXPERIENCING STATIC?)
QRN

(CHECK TEST SIGNAL)
10-97 ('Official' 10-Code)

(DISAPPEARANCE OR FADING OF SIGNAL)
dead spot
dropout

(DISTANT SIGNAL)
on skip
skip
skipland
skiptalk
trip

(GOOD, CLEAR SIGNAL)
five-by-five
five-five
getting out
making the trip
10-2 (Abbreviated 10-Code)

(INTERMITTENT SIGNAL)
breaking up
motorboating

(IS THE SIGNAL FADING?)
QBS

(IS YOUR SET OPERATING?)
How about your vocal chords? (SE)

(OVERPOWERED BY STRONGER SIGNAL)
stepped on
walked all over
walked on
walking on you
wiped out
zapped

(SIGNAL INTERFERENCE)
bleed over
bleeding
buckshot
covered up
garbage
hash
in the mud
jammed out
splatter
stepped on
trampled

(SIGNAL TOO STRONG)
bleeding (NW)
block
bomb
coming in too torrible (SE)
melting the voice coil

(SIGNAL UNCLEAR)
covered up

(SIGNAL UNCLEAR—*continued*)
hash and trash (W)

(STRONG SIGNAL)
armchair copy
forty-over
hot 'n heavy

(WEAK SIGNAL)
10-1 (Abbreviated 10-Code)
thin (NW)

RAILROAD CONDUCTOR
shack

RAIN (see WEATHER CONDITIONS)

RECEPTION (see also RADIO SIGNAL)

(BACKGROUND NOISE)
background
background too heavy
hash and trash
mud

(CAN ONLY HEAR ONE PERSON OF CONVERSATION)
ghost talking (S)

(CLEAR RECEPTION OF SIGNAL)
bending the windows (SE)
big ears
blowing smoke
bodacious (SE)
breaking the old needle (SE)
burning up my ears
coming in loud and proud (SE)
coming out of the windows (SE)
dig you out
five-and-nine
five-by-nine

(CLEAR RECEPTION—*continued*)
got a 10-2
hang my needle
in the clear
make the trip
pinnin' the needle
pull you out
shaking the windows (W)
sounding choice
10-2 ('Official' 10-Code)
walking in here blowing smoke (SE)
walking the dog
wall-to-wall
wall-to-wall and treetop tall (W)
wall-to-wall, ten feet tall (SE)
you're looking good

(GIVE ME A LONG COUNT)
10-94 ('Official' 10-Code)

(HOW ARE YOU RECEIVING MY SIGNAL?)
QRK

(HOW DO YOU RECEIVE MY TRANS-
MISSION?)
How am I hitting you?

(IS TRANSMISSION RECEIVED?)
Make the trip?

(RECEIVING POORLY)
10-1 ('Official' 10-Code)

(TURN ANTENNA FOR BETTER RECEPTION)
turning my house around (W)

RESIDENCE (see HOME — LOCATION)

RESTAURANT
bean store
chew and choke

RESTAURANT *(continued)*
  chowdown
  coffee pot
  eatum-up-stop
  juke joint

RESTROOM (see also STOPS)
  catbox
  sandbox
  ten-hundred room

REYNOLDSBURG, OHIO
  Tomato Town (MW)

RHODE ISLAND
  Mini State (NE)

ROAD (see also LANE)
  boulevard (SE)

  (AREA OF ROAD NOT VISIBLE TO DRIVER)
  blind

  (ADVISE ROAD CONDITIONS)
  10-13 (Abbreviated and 'Official' 10-Codes)

  (BUMPY ROAD)
  loose boardwalk
  washboard

  (CROWDED HIGHWAY)
  four lane parking lot (W)

  (CURVE IN ROAD)
  licorice stick
  nerve curve
  snake

  (EXPRESSWAY OR HIGHWAY)
  big slab (SE)
  boulevard
  concrete jungle (W)

(EXPRESSWAY—*continued*)
pike
rip strip
super slab

(HIGHWAY CLOVERLEAF)
mixing bowl
mix-master
twister

(ICY OR SLIPPERY ROAD)
greasy (NE)
skating rink
slip and slide (SE)
slick like slime on a doorknob (MW)

(INTERSECTION — CONFUSING)
mix-master (SW)

(INTERSTATE 55)
double nickel highway (SE)

(INTERSTATE 90 IN OHIO)
radar alley

(OTHER SIDE OF THE ROAD)
flip
flip-flop

(ROAD AHEAD)
front yard

(ROAD BEHIND)
backyard
over the shoulder

(ROAD UNDER CONSTRUCTION)
flag city (or town)

(ROAD WHERE CONDITIONS CAUSE INTER-
FERENCE WITH CB)
tunnel of love

(ROAD WITH MANY SPEED TRAPS)
boulevard of broken dreams

(SHORT STRETCH OF ROAD)
driveway

(SOFT BLACKTOP ON ROAD)
fly paper

(TOLL ROAD)
green stamp road

(YELLOW STRIPE ON ROAD)
banana peel

ROAD CLEAR OF POLICE AND OBSTRUCTIONS;
  DRIVE DESIRED SPEED
     bring it on
     bring yourself on in (SE)
     brought it on
     clean
     clean and green (SW)
     clean as a hound's tooth (SE)
     clean shot (SE)
     clear as a spring day (SE)
     clear shot
     drop the hammer down
     everything is slick
     friendly territory
     good shot
     green light
     green light and a white line
     haven't seen a thing in your lane
     if you got the desire, set your wheels on fire
     knock it about
     land of wonderful (SE)
     let the hammer down
     light's green
     light's green, bring on the machine
     nothing but a green light and a white line

ROAD CLEAR OF POLICE *(continued)*

 put the pedal to the metal and let it roar (MW)
 put your pedal to the metal and have yourself a
  ball 'cause in that *north*bound lane we haven't
  seen nothin' at all
 put yourself up here (SE)
 slick and clear as a spring day
 slick like slime on a doorknob
 straight shot (SE)
 way is bueno (SE)
 we're clear
 we're out
 we're out of it

 (IS THE ROAD CLEAR?)
 How we be looking back your way?

ROAD CONSTRUCTION WORKER
 flag-waver
 gandy dancer

ROANOKE, VIRGINIA
 Star City

ROCHESTER, MINNESOTA
 Doctor Town

ROCK ISLAND, ILLINOIS
 The Rock

ROOM — RESERVE ROOM FOR _____
 10-82 ('Official' 10-Code)

ROOM WHERE CB IS INSTALLED
 shack

ROSWELL, NEW MEXICO
 Cactus Patch (SW)

RURAL AREA
 boondocks

RURAL AREA *(continued)*
    boonies

ST. LOUIS, MISSOURI
    Big Arch
    Budweiser City
    Busch City
    Gateway (The)
    Gateway City (MW)
    Gateway to the West
    Golden Archways

ST. PAUL/MINNEAPOLIS, MINNESOTA
    Twin Cities

SALT LAKE CITY, UTAH
    Big Salty

SAN ANGELO, TEXAS
    Trash Town (SW)

SAN ANTONIO, TEXAS
    Alamo City (or Town) (SW)
    River City (SW)
    Taco Town

SAN CLEMENTE, CALIFORNIA
    Tricky Dick's (W)

SAN DIEGO, CALIFORNIA
    Dago
    S.D.
    Swabby Town

SAN FRANCISCO, CALIFORNIA
    Bay City (W)
    Frisco
    Hill Town
    Quake City

SARASOTA, FLORIDA
Circus City

SARATOGA, NEW YORK
Toga Town

SCHOOL — LOCATION
school twenty

SEATTLE, WASHINGTON
Needle City

SEE (see LOOK)

SEXUAL ACTIVITY
clean up
little bit (SE, SW)

SHAKE HANDS
gimme five

SHERIFF'S DEPARTMENT (see LAW ENFORCE-
MENT)

SHOWER
run through the raindrops (NE)

SHOWER ROOM
rain locker (W)

SHREVEPORT, LOUISIANA
Sport City (SE)

SIGN-OFF (see also BEST WISHES; DRIVE
SAFELY)
a little here, a little there, you gotta watch out for
Smokey the Bear
adios (SW)
big eights
big threes
catcha later (MW)
clear

SIGN-OFF *(continued)*

clear after you
clear and rolling (SE)
clear there with you (SE)
cut loose
do it to it like Sonny Pruitt
doin' it to it, that way (SE)
doing our thing in the lefthand lane (SE)
don't let your tricking trip up your trucking (SE)
don't let your trucking trip up your tricking (SE)
down
down and gone
down and out of it
*east*bound, struttin' style
*east*bound, trailer truckin' style
eights
eights and other good numbers
eighty-eights
eighty-eights around the house
going down
going thataway
gone
good pair
have a 36-24-36 tonight
have yourself a good day today and a better day
    tomorrow
I'm through
in the clear
keep on trucking
keep the antenna wigglin' and the girls gigglin'
keep the beavers in your lap and the bears off
    your back and have yourself a fine day (NE)
keep the bugs off the glass and the bears off
    your tail
keep the rolling side down down and the shiny
    side up

SIGN-OFF *(continued)*

keep the rubber side down

keep the shiny side up and the dirty side down (NW)

keep the shiny side up and the greasy side down

keep the shiny side up and the rolling side down

keep your nose between the ditches and smokey out of your britches

keep your wheels out of the ditches and the smokeys out of your britches

keep your wheels spinning and the beavers grinning

may all your and downs be between the sheets

nothing but a green light and a white line

o.k.

pepsi day

put your pedal to the metal and have yourself a ball 'cause in that *north*bound lane we haven't seen nothin' at all

seven threes

seventy-thirds to you

smokey's off the road, smokey's in the grass, smokey's out raking leaves, but we've got CBs (SE)

stay between the jumps and bumps

stay between the jumps and the bumps and truck over all the humps

subsequently or indirectly we'll catch you come lately on the frequently, 10-4?

ten bye-bye

ten-ten 'til we do it again

thirty-twelve

threes and eights

we be toppin' these hills and poppin' these pills

we down, we gone, bye-bye

we go

SIGN-OFF *(continued)*

we go bye-bye (MW)
we gone
we quit
we up, we down, we clear, we gone
we up, we down, we out, we gone
we went
we're backing 'em up now
we're clear
we're down (SE)
we're out
we're out of it
*west*bound and just lookin' around

(END OF TRANSMISSION) (see also OFF — TURNING OFF THE CB; TRANSMIT)
bow out
clear
cut loose
down
down and gone
out
over and out
pull the big one
pull the big switch

(THROUGH TRANSMITTING BUT MONITORING) (see also LISTEN)
down and on the side
down, out, and on the side
he's layin', he's stayin'
lay it over (SE)
over
play dead
10-10 ('Official' 10-Code)
we gone
we're down, out, on the side (SE)

SIGNAL (see RADIO SIGNAL)

SIOUX FALLS, SOUTH DAKOTA
    The Sioux

SIPHON HOSE
    Arkansas credit card

SKATEBOARD
    four-wheeled log

SLEEP (GO TO BED)
    cut some Z's
    get horizontal (W)
    hit the hay
    hit the rack
    hit the sheets (SE)
    hit the snore shelf
    log some Z's
    nod out
    press some sheets (SW)

    (BED)
    rack
    snore shelf
    trampoline
    wave maker (water bed)

    (SLEEPING)
    down for the count (NE)
    flat side
    horizontal
    horizontally polarized
    Z's-ville (NE)

    (VERY TIRED)
    draggin' it out behind (SW)
    making three tracks in the sand (SW)

SLOW; SLOWING DOWN (see SPEED)

SMOKE; FIRE
hot pants

SNOW (see WEATHER CONDITIONS)

SNOWMOBILE ENTHUSIAST
sled head

SOON
in a short, short (SE)

SOUTH BEND, INDIANA
Irish City

SPEECH DIFFICULTY
baryphony

SPEED (see also DRIVE; ROAD CLEAR OF POLICE
AND OBSTRUCTIONS)

(ACCELERATE)
cover ground
drop the hammer down
get trucking
hammer down
hammer hanging
hammer on (NE)
highball
jack it up (SE)
knock the slack out (SE)
let it go (MW)
let it roll
let the hammer down
let the motor tote 'er
let the pedal hit the metal (SE)
pedal against the metal (SE)
pedal down
pedal to the metal
pour on (the) coal

(ACCELERATE—*continued*)

put one foot on the floor, hang your toenails on
   the radiator, and let the motor tote 'er

put the hammer down

put the pedal to the floor

put the pedal to the metal

put the pedal to the metal and let it roar

put your foot on the floor and let the motor tote
   'er (SE)

put your pedal to the metal and let your motor
   tote 'er

shovel coal (SE)

smoke on brother (SE)

smoke some dope (SE)

tighten up on the rubberband (SE)

(DESIRED SPEED)

cooking good

tooling along

(DRIVING SLOWLY, UNABLE TO SEE PROP-
ERLY)

pedaling dead and blind

(EXCEED SPEED LIMIT SLIGHTLY TO FLUSH
OUT HIDDEN POLICE)

smoke 'em out

(55 MPH)

doing the five-five

double nickel

driving the peg

double buffalo

double fiver

five-five

fives-a-pair

legalized

light footin' it

(55 MPH—*continued*)

pair of fives
pair of nickels

(FULL SPEED)
both feet on the floor
diggin' my spurs
do it to it
doin' it to it (SE)
doing our thing in the lefthand lane
*east*bound struttin' style
ginning and got the wheels spinning (SE)
got his shoes on (SE)
got my foot on it (SE)
lay it to the floor
let the hammer down
light's green, bring on the machine
one foot on the floor, one hanging out the door,
    and she just won't do no more (SE)
pedaling with both feet
put it on the floor and looking for some more
    (SE)
rubberband going (SE)
scratchin'
streaking (MW)
tighten your seat down, we're running heavy
toenails are scratching (SE)
toenails in the radiator (SE)
toenails on the front bumper (SE)

(LEGAL SPEED) (see also SPEED — 55 MPH)
light footin' it
on the pay
on the peg

(MOVING FAST)
foot in the carburetor

(MOVING FAST—*continued*)
highballing
on the fly
pedal against the metal (SE)
pedal down
pushin' it
smoking
spittin' and gettin' (SW)

(60 MPH)
on the sixty

(SLOW DOWN)
back down
back 'em off
back 'em on down (or up) (SE)
back 'em up (SE)
back off
back off on it (SE)
back off the hammer (SE, W)
back on down (SE)
back out of it
better cool it
brush your teeth and comb your hair (NW)
flaps down
hammer back
hammer off (NE)
hammer up
legalize
let your flaps down (SE)
95 is the route you're on, it's not the speed limit
    sign (NE, SE)
pedal a little slower (SE)
pull in them reins
pull your hammer back (SW)
put the hammer in the tool box
toss the hammer back in the 'ol tool box (SE)

(SLOW DOWN—*continued*)
use the jake (SW)
we're backing 'em up now (SE)

(SLOWING DOWN OR STOPPING)
sliding my wheels (NW)

(VEHICLE VARYING SPEED)
yo yo (SE)

SPOUSE (see also HUSBAND; WIFE)
X-Y
X-Y-L
X-Y-O (NW)

SPRINGFIELD, MISSOURI
Queen City (MW)

SPRINGFIELD, TENNESSEE
Tobacco Capitol

STAND BY (see also MONITOR)
10-6 ('Official' 10-Code)
10-12 (Abbreviated 10-Code)
10-23 ('Official' 10-Code)

STATE TROOPER (see LAW ENFORCEMENT)

STOLEN MERCHANDISE
five-finger discount

(BUYING OR SELLING STOLEN CB RADIO
OR EQUIPMENT)
225 sale

(STOLEN CB RADIO)
rig rip-off

STOP DRIVING (see DRIVING)

STOP TRANSMITTING (see SIGN-OFF; TRANS-
MIT)

STOPPED; PARKED (see also DRIVING)
> dozing
> in the pan

> (PULLED OVER OR ARRESTED BY POLICE)
> (see also DRIVER; TICKET)
> in the hole

> (STOPPED BECAUSE OF BROKEN-DOWN
> VEHICLE) (see also TRAFFIC ACCIDENT)
> lame
> on the side

STOPS (PLACES) (see also HOTEL)
> pit stop
> rest 'em up place (SE)
> turkey area
> water hole (SW)

> (EATING STOP — RESTAURANT)
> bean store
> bean wagon
> chew and choke
> chowdown
> coffee pot
> eatum-up-stop
> pit stop
> stop to get groceries (SW)

> (GAS OR FUEL STOP)
> pit stop

> (RESTROOM STOP)
> choking a chicken (MW)
> coke stop (SW)
> drain the radiator (NE)
> go 10-100 (W)
> nature break (SE)
> nature call (MW)
> pause for a cause

(RESTROOM STOP—*continued*)
pit stop
play in the sandbox
pull in for a short, short (SE)
scratch the sandbox (MW)
short, short
ten-one hundred (10-100) (SW, W)
wipe the mirror (NE)
wipe the windshield (NE)

(TRUCK STOP)
oasis
stage stop (SW)
truck 'em up stop
waterhole (SW)

STRATFORD, CONNECTICUT
Shakespeare Town (NE)

SUPERIOR, WISCONSIN
Little Twin
Twin Fort

TALK (see CB CONVERSATION; TRANSMIT)

TALK TOO CLOSE TO THE MIKE (see TRANSMIT)

TAMPA, FLORIDA
Big T
Cigar City

TAXICAB
hack

TAXPAYER
loser (NE)

TEENAGER
bubblegummer

TELEPHONE
Channel 25 (NE)

TELEPHONE *(continued)*

    double "L"
    land line
    T-X
    twisted pair

    (CALL BY TELEPHONE)
    10-21 (Abbreviated and 'Official' 10-Codes)

    (MOBILE TELEPHONE)
    clothesline (MW)

    (MY TELEPHONE NUMBER IS _____)
    10-84 ('Official' 10-Code)

    (TELEPHONE PATCH)
    lima

TELEPHONE OR POWER LINES ACROSS ROAD
    clothesline

TELEPHONE POLES
    toothpicks (MW)

TELEVISION
    boob tube
    idiot box
    monster
    one-eyed monster

TELEVISION INTERFERENCE CAUSED BY CB
  TRANSMISSION
    T-V-I
    10-90 ('Official' 10-Code)
    Tennessee Valley Indians

TENNESSEE
    Volunteer State

TEXARKANA, ARKANSAS
    T Town (SE)

TEXARKANA, TEXAS
> T Town (SW)

TEXAS
> Longhorn State

THIEF
> chicken snatcher (MW)
> midnight shopper

TICKET (see also DRIVER — WHO IS CAUGHT SPEEDING; TRAFFIC FINE)

> (AVOID GETTING SPEEDING TICKET)
> don't feed the bears
> keep the beavers in your lap and the bears off your back
> keep the bugs off the glass and the bears off your tail
> keep your nose between the ditches and smokey out of your britches
> keep your wheels out of the ditches and the smokeys out of your britches
> starve the bears

> (DRIVER GIVEN A SPEEDING TICKET)
> bit by the bear
> bit on the seat of the britches (SE)
> feeding the bears

> (NOTICE OF VIOLATION OF FCC RULES)
> pink ticket

> (POLICE GIVING OUT SPEEDING TICKETS)
> bagging them (NE)
> spreading the greens (SE)

> (SPEEDING TICKET)
> bear bite (SE)
> blue slip (SW)

(SPEEDING TICKET—*continued*)
Christmas card (NE)
coupon (SE)
extra money ticket (W)
green stamps
greens (SE)
paperwork (SE)
piece of paper

(TRAFFIC TICKET)
invitation
paper

(WARNING TICKET)
pink QSL card (SW, W)
pink slip (SW, W)

TIGHTEN CHAINS HOLDING DOWN CARGO
boom it down

TIME

(BEHIND TIME)
off stop watch (MW)
strapped for time

(CORRECT TIME)
QTR
10-34 (Abbreviated 10-Code)
10-36 ('Official' 10-Code)

(DEPARTURE TIME)
QTN

(ESTIMATED TIME OF ARRIVAL)
QRE
10-26 (Abbreviated 10-Code)
time on the dime

(ON TIME)
on the stop watch (MW)

TIRED
   checking my eyelids for pin holes (W)

TIRES
   balloon tires (radial tires)
   baloneys
   feet
   floats
   skins
   tennis shoes

   (CHECK THE TIRES)
   kick the donuts

   (TIRE TROUBLE)
   blown pumpkin
   bubble trouble
   pumpkin
   rags
   slick tennis shoes
   sore feet (MW)

   (TRUCK TIRES)
   donuts

TOLEDO, OHIO
   Scale City

TOLL BOOTH
   cash register
   green stamp (NE)
   piggy bank (NE, MW)

TOLL ROAD (see ROAD)

TOP OF THE CONTINENTAL DIVIDE (DENVER, COLORADO)
   Loveland Pass

TOW TRUCK (see TRUCK — WRECKER)

TOWN (see also CITY)
    old (*town name*) town
    patch

TRAFFIC
    rat race
    tense

    (TRAFFIC JAM)
    gaper's block
    parking lot
    stall ball

    (LOCATION OF TRAFFIC JAM)
    10-43 ('Official' 10-Code)

TRAFFIC ACCIDENT
    bang 'em up
    fender bender

    (LOCATION OF TRAFFIC ACCIDENT)
    10-42 ('Official' 10-Code)

    (VEHICLE TURNED OVER; WRECK)
    belly up
    fender bender

TRAFFIC COURT
    train station

TRAFFIC FINE
    county mounty bounty

TRANSMIT; TRANSMISSION (see also CB CONVERSATION)

    (ACTIVATE THE MIKE)
    key
    keying the mike
    squashing the key

    (ACTIVATE THE MIKE WITHOUT SPEAKING)
    buttonpushing

(ACTIVATE MIKE WITHOUT SPEAKING—*cont.*)
dropping a carrier
10-95 ('Official' 10-Code)

(ANOTHER TURN AT TRANSMITTING)
go 'round

(CAUSING INTERFERENCE)
10-75 ('Official' 10-Code)

(INTERRUPTED TRANSMISSION)
bruising my body
dusted your ears (SE)
stepped all over you (SE)
whomping on you (SE)

(KEYING AND UNKEYING MIKE RAPIDLY)
three-fiving the mike (NE)

(KEYING MIKE TO PREVENT TRANSMISSION)
blocking the channel (SE)
buttonpushing
dropped a carrier on us
jam
mashing the mike (SE)

(LAST TRANSMISSION)
final

(PROCEED WITH TRANSMISSION IN SE-
QUENCE)
10-71 ('Official' 10-Code)

(SIDEBAND)
L-S-B (lower sideband)
S-S-B (single sideband)
slider (NW)
U-S-B (upper sideband)

(STOP TRANSMITTING) (see also OFF —
TURNING OFF THE CB; SIGN-OFF)
back 'em on down (or up)
back 'em up

(STOP TRANSMITTING—*continued*)
back it on out
back off
back on down
back out
back out of it
clear
clear there with you (SE)
cut loose (SE)
down
gone
I'm through
out
10-3 (Abbreviated and 'Official' 10-Codes)
10-7 (Abbreviated and 'Official' 10-Codes)
we go
we went

(TALKING TOO CLOSE TO THE MIKE)
overmodulation

(TALKING TOO LONG)
overmodulation
rachet jawing

(TALKING TOO RAPIDLY)
10-11 ('Official 10-Code)

(TALKING WITH MIKE CLOSE TO MOUTH)
close-talk

(TRANSMISSION OUT OF ADJUSTMENT)
10-92 ('Official' 10-Code)

(TRANSMISSION UNCLEAR)
mushy

(TRANSMITTING OVER LONG DISTANCE)
skiptalk
talking skip

(TRANSMIT LONG DISTANCE—*continued*)
walking the dog
we're trying

(UNEVEN TRANSMISSION)
wrinkle (SE)

(WEAK TRANSMISSION, SURROUNDED BY STRONGER SIGNAL)
peanut butter three

TRAVELING (see DRIVING)

TRIP

(DRIVER'S FIRST TRIP IN NEW TRUCK)
honeymoon

(EASY TRIP)
milk run

(ENROUTE)
10-17 (Abbreviated 10-Code)

(LONG HAUL TRIP)
expressway boogie

(RETURN TRIP)
backslide (SE)
backstroke (SE)
bounce-around (SE)
flip
flip-flop
flipper
on a (*name of city*) turn (SE)
rebound
rewind (NE)

(ROUND TRIP)
turn-around

(SHORT HAUL TRIP)
cream puff

(SPEAK TO YOU ON THE RETURN TRIP)
catch you on the flipper
catch you on the old flip-flop
catch you on the reverse

TRUCK (see also IDENTIFICATION)
rig
transporter
unit

(ARMORED TRUCK)
branch bank

(AUTO CARRIER)
mobile parking lot (W)
movable parking deck
portable parking lot (SE)

(BEER TRUCK)
honey wagon (SE)

(CEMENT TRUCK)
muck truck

(CINDER TRUCK)
salt shaker

(EMPTY TRUCK)
load of post holes

(FLATBED TRACTOR TRAILER)
flat back
flatbed
portable floor (SE)

(GARBAGE TRUCK)
roach coach

(GRAVEL AND TAR TRUCK)
pepper shaker (NE)

(HEARSE)
box on wheels
one-way camper (NE)

(HIGHWAY REPAIR TRUCK)
flag-waver taxi

(ICE CREAM EXPRESS)
I-C-X

(MILK TANKER)
portable cow (SW)
portable pipeline
thermos bottle

(MOVING VAN)
bedbug hauler
relocation consultants

(OLD TRUCK)
iron

(PICK-UP TRUCK)
cowboy cadillac (MW)
pick 'em up truck
pickdown (MW)
pickum-up

(REFRIGERATED TRUCK)
reefer

(SAND TRUCK)
salt shaker (NE)
sand blaster

(SLEEPING AREA IN TRACTOR CAB)
coffin (NE)
coffin box
pajama wagon
sleeper
suicide sleeper

(SMALL TRUCK)
city flyer
four-by-four
four-wheeler

(SMALL TRUCK—*continued*)
pickum-up
six-wheeler

(SNOWPLOW)
pathfinder
salt shaker (NE)

(STREET-CLEANING TRUCK)
scrub brush

(TRACTOR TRAILER TRUCK)
big car
big rig
box (SE)
bucket of bolts (MW)
country cadillac (SE)
diesel car
eighteen-legged pogo stick (MW)
eighteen-wheeler
forty-footer
growed up truck (SE)
horse (MW)
old kitty whomper (MW)
set of doubles

(TRAILER OR CONTAINER CARRIED BY
RAIL)
piggy bank

(TRUCK CAB — HIGH)
cherry picker

(TRUCK CARRYING FREIGHT CONTAINER
TO OR FROM AIRCRAFT)
birdyback

(TRUCK CARRYING MOBILE HOME)
shanty shaker
wobbly box

(TRUCK CARRYING OVERLOAD)
fat daddy

(TRUCK HAULING ANIMALS)
bull rack (NW)

(TRUCK HAULING BEVERAGES)
bottle popper

(TRUCK HAULING BRICKS)
load of rocks (NW)

(TRUCK HAULING CATTLE)
Polack school bus
portable stock yard

(TRUCK HAULING DANGEROUS CARGO)
boom wagon

(TRUCK HAULING FRUITS AND VEGE-
TABLES)
bean hauler

(TRUCK HAULING GAS, OIL, OR LIQUID;
TANKER)
petro refinery (SW)
Polish hairtonic
portable barnyard
portable can
portable gas station
portable pipeline
rolling refinery (SW)
soda fountain
tanker
thermos bottle

(TRUCK HAULING LUMBER)
load of sticks (NW)

(TRUCK HAULING POULTRY)
barnyard
cackle crate
chicken choker

(TRUCK MADE FANCY)
goodied up

(TRUCK — MANUFACTURER)
Bulldog (Mack)
Fix Or Repair Daily (Ford)
Corn Binder (International Truck) (NW)
Fruitliner (White)
Hillbilly Wagon (White)
Jimmie (General Motors)
K-Whomper (Kenworth) (NE)
Kitty Whomper (Kenworth) (NE)
Pete (Peterbilt)
Polack Peterbilt (International Harvester) (MW)

(TRUCK TRACTOR PULLING TRAILER(S))
choo-choo train
double-trouble (NE)
peanut wagon

(TRUCK TRAILER)
bushel basket
house

(TRUCK WITH A FLAT TIRE)
seventeen-wheeler

(TRUCK WITH LOW POWER OR NOT RUN-
NING PROPERLY)
dog
sick horse

(TRUCK TRACTOR — WITHOUT A TRAILER)
bareback tractor
bobtail
cab
tractor
van

(TRUCKING COMPANY TRUCK)
Big Blue-Eyed Indian (Navajo Freight Lines) (NW)
Big Orange (Synder)
Big R (Roadway Freight System)
Corn Flake (Consolidated Freightway)
Halloween Machine (Cooper-Jarrett Trucking Company)
Portable Road Block (McLean Trucking)
Safer Shaffer (Shaffer Trucking)
Snuffy Smith (Smith Transfer Company) (NE)
Super Chicken (Yellow Freight)

(TWO TRACTOR TRAILER TRUCKS DRIVING SIDE BY SIDE)
double 18

(UNCOMFORTABLE OR NOISY TRUCK)
cement mixer
kidney buster

(WRECKER)
draggin' wagon
Tijuana taxi (MW)

TRUCK DRIVER (see DRIVER)

TRUCK ENGINE (see ENGINE)

TRUCK EMITTING BLACK SMOKE
smoker
smudge pot

TRUCK MOVING SLOWLY UPHILL
pushmobile

TRUCK ROUTE WITH MANY STOPS
peddle run

TRUCK TRAILER TIPPED FORWARD
    nose dive

TRUCK WHEELS
    P-F flyers (SE)

TRUCKERS' HANGOUT
    candy store

TRUCKERS' LOG SHEETS
    comic books
    lie sheets
    swindle sheets

TUCSON, ARIZONA
    Big T (SW)

TUNNEL
    hole in the wall

TURN RIGHT (or LEFT) (see also DIRECTION)
    hang a right (or left) (MW)
    peel off (SE)

U-TURN (see DIRECTION; TRIP)

UNCOUPLE TRACTOR FROM TRAILER
    break the unit

UNDER THE HOOD OF A VEHICLE
    in (or under) the doghouse

UNDERSTAND (see also YES)
    dig you out (SE)
    pull you out

    (CAN'T UNDERSTAND)
    can't pull you out
    covered up
    negative copy

(CAN'T UNDERSTAND — USE TELEPHONE)
10-62 ('Official' 10-Code)

(DO YOU UNDERSTAND?)
Copy?
Dig?
Dig it?
Do you copy?
Do you have a copy?
Do you read me?
Forty-D?
Four?
Got the copy?
Rodgie?
Roger?
Roger-D?
Roger-dodger?
Ten-fer?
Ten-four?
Ten roger?

(HARD TO UNDERSTAND)
hard to pull out

URGENT
10-17 ('Official' 10-Code)
10-18 (Abbreviated 10-Code)

VAN
art cart
micro bus (MW)

(CAMPER)
box
home on its back
turtle
waggin' tail

(CAMPER OR TRUCK PULLING MOBILE HOME)
portable massage parlor (MW)

(FANCY VAN)
luxury apartment on wheels (W)
movin' motel (W)

(MOBILE HOME TRAILER)
luxury apartment on wheels
movin' motel

(VOLKSWAGEN CAMPER)
bedbug (NE)

(VOLKSWAGEN VAN)
cracker box
pregnant skate board (NW)

VEHICLE (see also BUS; CAR; HELICOPTER;LAW ENFORCEMENT VEHICLE; LINE OF VEHICLES USING CB; MOTORCYCLE; TAXICAB; TRUCK; VAN)
mobile

(EMPTY VEHICLE)
shoulder boulder

(SLOW-MOVING VEHICLE) (see also DRIVER; SPEED)
boogie fever (SE)
dead pedal
grapefruit
pushmobile
rolling road block
sightseer
turtle (NE)

(VEHICLE ANNOYING OTHER DRIVERS)
porcupine

(VEHICLE EMITTING SMOKE)
oil burner

(VEHICLE GOING FIRST TO FLUSH OUT POLICE)
pacer

(VEHICLE LOW ON FUEL)
sinking ship

(VEHICLE NOT POLICE)
all clean
all washed out

(VEHICLE ON FIRE)
burning paint (MW)

(VEHICLE SPEEDING WITHOUT CB) (see also DRIVER; SPEED)
bear bait (SE)
bear bait passenger (SE)
bear food
bear meat
four-wheeler with fire in his tail
run interference

(VEHICLE WITH CB)
loaded for bear

(VEHICLE WITH LINEAR AMPLIFIER) (see also CB RADIO; CB USE)
Texas trunk

(VEHICLE WITH NO LIGHTS ON)
sleepin' peepers (MW)

(VEHICLE WITH ONE HEADLIGHT)
padiddle

(VEHICLE WITH SEVERAL ANTENNAS)
porcupine

(VEHICLE WITH TWO OR MORE AXLES)
bogey

(VEHICLE WITHOUT CB)
bareback (SW)

(VEHICLE WITHOUT CB—*continued*)
running Van Gogh

(VEHICLE WITHOUT CB FOLLOWING ONE
SO EQUIPPED)
bob-tailing
latch-on (SE)
rider (SE)
rumble seat

WEATHER CONDITIONS

(ADVISE WEATHER CONDITIONS)
10-13 (Abbreviated and 'Official' 10-Codes)

(FOG)
ground clouds

(HAIL)
popcorn

(RAIN)
cats and dogs (MW)
deep water
window washer

(SNOW)
confetti
dandruff
fluff stuff

WEIGH STATION (see also DRIVING — BACK ROADS AT NIGHT TO AVOID WEIGH STATION)
chicken coop
D.O.T.
portable chicken coop
scale house

(WEIGH STATION IS CLOSED)
chicken coop is clean
scale house is all right
scale house is clean

(WEIGH STATION WORKER)
chicken inspector
flight man (SE, SW, W)
weight man
weight watcher (W)

VOICE
modulation

WASHINGTON, D. C.
D.C.
Watergate City (or Town)

WASHINGTON STATE
Logging Capitol

WICHITA, KANSAS
Air Cap 8

WIFE
better half
first sergeant (W)
M-O-L (SW)
mama (SE)
O-W
old lady
other half
warden
X-Y-L
Y-F

(EX-WIFE)
X

WINCHESTER, VIRGINIA
Apple Capital (SE)
Apple City

WINDSHIELD WIPERS
slappers

WINSTON-SALEM, NORTH CAROLINA
    Tobacco City
    Twin City

WOMAN (see also PERSON; SPOUSE; WIFE)
    beaver
    chick (NE)
    cover (NE)
    foxy lady
    mini skirt (SE)
    muff
    postage stamp (NE)
    quasar
    super skirt
    sweet lady
    sweet thing
    wooly bear (SE)
    wooly-wooly (SE)

    (ATTRACTIVE WOMAN)
    foxy lady
    frilly blouse
    muffin
    seat cover
    wooly critter

    (BUM)
    hag bag

    (FAT WOMAN)
    two-stool beaver

    (GIRL BELOW LEGAL AGE OF CONSENT)
    jailbait
    quail
    San Quentin
    San Quentin jail bait (SE)

    (OLD WOMAN) (see also WIFE; SPOUSE)
    O-W

(STRIPPER)
split beaver

(UNATTRACTIVE FEMALE)
paperbag case (NE)

(UNMARRIED WOMAN)
X-L

(YOUNG WOMAN)
Y-L

WORK; WORKER (see also EMPLOYMENT LOCA-
TION)

(DAY WORKERS)
nine-to-fivers

(DOCKWORKER WHO UNLOADS FREIGHT)
dock-walloper

(INSTRUCTIONS GIVEN TO TRUCKER BY
DISPATCHER)
flying orders

(MAKE PICKUP AT _____)
10-16 ('Official' 10-Code)

(PICK-UPS AND DELIVERIES OF CARGO)
P & D's

(QUIT WORKING)
gunny bag (NW)
pack it up

(TRUCK-DRIVING JOB)
rig gig

(UNLOAD CARGO)
strip her

(WORKING MAN)
hard ankle

WORK ASSIGNMENT

(ALL UNITS COMPLY)
10-67 ('Official' 10-Code)

(ALL UNITS WITHIN RANGE — REPORT)
10-45 ('Official' 10-Code)

(ASSIGNMENT COMPLETED)
10-24 (Abbreviated and 'Official' 10-Codes)

(AWAITING NEXT MESSAGE/ASSIGNMENT)
10-65 ('Official' 10-Code)

(IN SERVICE)
10-8 (Abbreviated and 'Official' 10-Codes)

(MISSION COMPLETE   ALL UNITS SECURE)
10-99 ('Official' 10-Code)

(ON DUTY)
10-11 (Abbreviated 10-Code)

(RETURN TO BASE, NOTHING FOR YOU)
10-19 ('Official' 10-Code)

(UNITS NEEDED)
10-32 (Abbreviated 10-Code)

WRECKER (see TRUCK — WRECKER)

YES; I UNDERSTAND; OK

a big ten-four
absitively and posilutely (NE)
affirmative
Charlie
Charlie Brown
Charlie, Charlie
definitely
fer sure
five-two
for sure
forty-roger
four

YES; I UNDERSTAND; OK *(continued)*

    four D
    four roger
    4-10
    four-ten roger
    guarantold you
    positive
    positary
    rodgie (MW)
    roger
    roger-D
    roger-dodger
    ten-fer
    10-4 (Abbreviated and 'Official' 10-Codes)
    ten roger
    ungowa bwana (NW)
    wilco
    yo
    yoo

YOUNGSTOWN, OHIO
    Baseball City

'OFFICIAL' TEN-CODE

10-1	Receiving poorly
10-2	Receiving well
10-3	Stop transmitting
10-4	OK, message received
10-5	Relay message
10-6	Busy, stand by
10-7	Out of service, leaving air
10-8	In service, subject to call
10-9	Repeat message
10-10	Transmission complete, standing by
10-11	Talking too rapidly
10-12	Visitors present
10-13	Advise weather and road condition

10-16	Make pickup at _____
10-17	Urgent business
10-18	Anything for us?
10-19	Nothing for you, return to base
10-20	My location is _____
10-21	Call by telephone
10-22	Report in person to _____
10-23	Stand by
10-24	Completed last assignment
10-25	Can you contact _____?
10-26	Disregard last message
10-27	I am moving to channel ____
10-28	Identify your station
10-29	Time is up for contact
10-30	Does not conform to FCC rules
10-32	I will give you a radio check
10-33	EMERGENCY TRAFFIC AT THIS STATION
10-34	TROUBLE AT THIS STATION, NEED HELP
10-35	Confidential information
10-36	Correct time is _____
10-37	Wrecker needed at _____
10-38	Ambulance needed at _____
10-39	Your message delivered
10-41	Please tune to channel ____
10-42	Traffic accident at _____
10-43	Traffic tie-up at _____
10-44	I have a message for you
10-45	All units within range please report
10-46	Assist motorist
10-50	Break channel
10-60	What is next message number?
10-62	Unable to copy; use phone
10-63	Network directed to _____
10-64	Network clear

10-65	Awaiting your next message/assignment
10-67	All units comply
10-69	Message received
10-70	Fire at _____
10-71	Proceed with transmission in sequence
10-73	Speed trap at _____
10-74	Negative
10-75	You are causing interference
10-77	Negative contact
10-81	Reserve hotel room for _____
10-82	Reserve room for _____
10-84	My telephone number is _____
10-85	My address is _____
10-89	Radio repairman needed at _____
10-90	I have T.V.I.
10-91	Talk closer to the mike
10-92	Your transmission is out of adjustment
10-93	Check my frequency on this channel
10-94	Please give me a long count
10-95	Transmit dead carrier for five seconds
10-97	Check test signal
10-99	Mission completed, all units secure
10-200	Police needed at _____

ABBREVIATED 10-CODE

10-1	Signal weak
10-2	Signal good
10-3	Stop transmitting
10-4	Affirmative, OK
10-5	Relay to _____
10-6	Busy
10-7	Out of service
10-8	In service
10-9	Repeat
10-10	Negative
10-11	On duty

10-12	Stand by (stop)
10-13	Existing conditions
10-14	Message/information
10-15	Message delivered
10-16	Reply to message
10-17	Enroute
10-18	Urgent
10-19	(In) contact
10-20	Location
10-21	Call _____ by phone
10-22	Disregard
10-23	Arrived at scene
10-24	Assignment completed
10-25	Report to meet
10-26	Estimated arrival time
10-27	License/permit information
10-28	Ownership information
10-29	Records check
10-30	Danger/caution
10-31	Pickup
10-32	Units needed
10-33	Help me quickly
10-34	Time

Q-CODE

QRA	What station are you?
QRB	How far are you from me?
QRD	Where are you headed, and from where did you come?
QRE	What is your estimated time of arrival at _____ (*destination*)?
QRF	Are you returning to _____ (*location*)?
QRG	What is my exact frequency?
QRK	How are you receiving my signal?
QRL	Are you busy?
QRM	Are you experiencing interference?
QRN	Are you experiencing static?

QRT	Shall I stop transmitting?
QRU	Have you anything for me?
QRV	Are you ready?
QRX	Will you wait?
QSB	Is the signal fading?
QSL	Postcard confirms CB communication.
QSM	Shall I repeat my last message?
QSO	Can you communicate with _____?
QSY	Will you change to a different channel?
QTC	How many messages do you have for me?
QTH	What is your location?
QTN	At what time did you depart from _____ (location)?
QTO	Have you left port (the dock)?
QTP	Are you going to enter port (the dock)?
QTR	What is the correct time?
QTU	During what hours is your station open?
QTV	Shall I stand guard for you on (#) Mhz/KHz?
QTX	Will you keep your station open for further communication?
QUA	Do you have news of _____?

13-CODE Furnished by James Escue "The Blade" (copyright applied for)

13- 1 All units copy and think you're an idiot.

13- 2 Yes, I copy, but I'm ignoring you.

13- 3 You're beautiful when you're mad.

13- 4 Sorry about that, big fella.

13- 5 Same to you, Sam.

13- 6 OK, so I goofed, none of us are human.

13- 7 If you can't copy me, it's your fault, because I'm running 3000 watts.

13- 8 You sound so illiterate, your parents couldn't have been married.

13- 9 Are you running "ancient mary"?

13-10   I'd gladly help you out, but I don't know how you got here in the first place

13-11   Have you tried blowing your nose? It might clear your ears.

13-12   It sounds like you still have foot-in-mouth disease.

13-13   Your friends must have pinned your co-ax again.

13-14   I know now what an antenna with less than unity gain sounds like.

13-15   Why did you pay for a license if you only run 130 milliwatts?

13-16   The mouse running your generator must be tired.

13-17   The only reason you're able to go horizontal is because your antenna fell down.

13-18   If I could copy you, I'd be tempted to answer.

13-19   Are you talking into the back of your mike?

13-20   Is your mike clinking or is your upper plate loose again?

13-21   Good grief; are you being paid for the word?

13-22   If you had spoke for another 30 seconds you would've been eligible for a broadcasting station license.

13-23   You made more sense the last time you were smashed.

13-24   Either my receiver is out of alignment, or you're on Channel 28.

13-25   That's a new antenna? I could get a better signal from a damn string.

13-26   What a fantastic signal, give me a few minutes so I can bring the mobile unit into your driveway so I can copy your message.

NEW TERMS

If you encounter new terms in your own use of the CB, or if you have any variations of those within this reference, please fill out the form below and send to the address noted at the bottom of the page.

TERM	MEANING	AREA
_____	_____	___
_____	_____	___
_____	_____	___
_____	_____	___
_____	_____	___
_____	_____	___
_____	_____	___
_____	_____	___
_____	_____	___
_____	_____	___

Send to:
Lanie Dills
P.O. Box 1444
Nashville, Tennessee 37202